HUMMINGBIRDS

HUMMINGBIRDS

Andrew Cleave

Dorset Press
New York

Title page photograph:
A recently fledged Black-chinned hummingbird in Arizona.

This edition published 1990 by
Dorset Press, a division of Marboro Books Corporation
ISBN 0-88029-370-5

Copyright © The Hamlyn Publishing Group Limited, 1989

This book was designed and produced by
The Hamlyn Publishing Group Limited,
a Division of the Octopus Publishing Group,
Michelin House, 81 Fulham Road,
London SW3 6RB, England

Produced by Mandarin Offset
Printed and bound in Hong Kong

CONTENTS

CHAPTER I

INTRODUCTION

The earliest records

Distribution and migration

Evolution and the spread of hummingbirds

Classification · Conservation

The male Ruby-throated hummingbird has a brilliantly colored gorget.

THE EARLIEST RECORDS

The English colonists who saw a hummingbird for the first time in the sixteenth century were in no doubt that what they were looking at was a tiny bird, although they would certainly have seen nothing like it in Europe. The Ruby-throated hummingbird, which they would have encountered when they first landed on the east coast of the United States, must have seemed one of the strangest sights of their new world. Indeed, it was often recorded in early writings as one of the wonders of the continent.

Writing in 1632, Thomas Morton describes the Ruby-throated hummingbird as a 'curious bird, . . . , no bigger than a great beetle; that out of question lives upon the bee, which hee eateth and catcheth amongst flowers. For it is his custom to frequent these places.' Morton observed the Ruby-throated hummingbird carefully and made what must have been the first real attempt to describe the habitat and way of life of this remarkable creature. He goes on to describe how he reckoned it obtained its food and also draws attention to the tiny bird's remarkable iridescent plumage; 'Flowers he cannot feed upon by reason of his sharp bill which is like the poynt of a Spanish needle, but shorte. His fethers have a gloss like silke, and as hee stirres they show to be a chaingable coloure; and has bin, and is admired for shape, coloure and size.'

Its small size, dazzling colours, incredible flying skills, and above all its humming sounds must have puzzled the early observers greatly. In 1634 William Wood described the Ruby-throated hummingbird as ' . . . one of the wonders of the Countrey, being no bigger than a Hornet, yet hath all the demensions of a Bird, as bill, and wings, with quills, spider-like legges, small clawes; for colour she is as glorious as the Raine-bow; as she flies, she makes a little humming noise like a Humble-bee; wherefore she is called the Humbird.'

The Ruby-throated hummingbird does produce a very audible humming sound when in flight, and it is for this reason that the whole family has been given the collective name of hummingbirds. Other species are far quieter, or have other distinguishing features, so if the English settlers had come across the Sword-billed hummingbird or the Purple thornbill first, the whole family might have had quite a different name. The male Broad-tailed hummingbird, of the Rockies and Great Basin mountains, produces a loud, trilling whistle rather than a hum, so we might have ended up with a name like 'whistling birds' if this species had been the first to be recorded.

In South America different names are used but they are still appropriate and descriptive. The Spanish name 'pica flor' or 'the flower picker' beautifully describes the method of feeding, while the Portuguese name 'beija flor' or 'the flower kisser', used in Brazil, is even more attractive. The French 'oiseau-mouches', meaning 'birds like flies', may refer to their small size, the insect-like humming sounds produced by the wings, or the way they hover around flowers. It may also refer to their fly-catching activities.

The early zoologists named the hummingbirds according to their physical appearance, often working from the skins of dead birds brought to their universities in Europe. Those who were fortunate enough to watch the birds in their natural habitats chose names that reflected the habits and appearance of the living bird. There are, therefore, several sylphs, woodnymphs, fairies and sunangels among the other, more color-related names which refer to the often dazzling plumage.

DISTRIBUTION AND MIGRATION

There are about 320 species of hummingbirds known to us today, all of them found in the Americas. The great majority occur in South America, and they are especially numerous in Ecuador and northern Brazil. A zone about ten degrees wide straddling the equator supports about half of the world's hummingbird species. The greater the distance from the equator, the smaller the number and variety of hummingbirds to be found. In Costa Rica, a small but mountainous country with a good range of habitats from mangrove swamps to mountain tops, there are 54 species, but Mexico, a far larger country at a greater distance from the equator, supports only 51. Twelve species manage to breed on the mainland of the United States, mostly west of the Rockies. East of the Mississippi only one species, the Ruby-throated hummingbird, is regularly found breeding. Similarly, in the far south of South America

The first hummingbird to be seen by the English colonists on their arrival in America was the Ruby-throated.

only one species, the Green-backed firecrown, is a regular breeder. It is faced with a long migration north at the end of each breeding season when the southern winter sets in.

THE DENSITY OF SPECIES OF HUMMINGBIRDS

1 species present

2–10 species present

11–50 species present

51–100 species present

over 100 species present

equator

The hummingbirds have managed to colonize practically the whole of North and South America, apart from the polar regions. Tropical rainforests support the greatest variety and abundance of these birds, but they can also be found in farmland, parks and gardens, orchards, arid deserts, coastal mangrove swamps, the coniferous forests of Canada and Alaska, and even the snow-clad slopes of the high Andes. Any habitat that offers a plentiful supply of flowers in bloom and a variety of insects will support hummingbirds.

The very small size of most hummingbirds does not mean that they are delicate birds incapable of withstanding difficult conditions. Some are able to live high up in the Andes, where night-time temperatures regularly fall below freezing and where the air is thin and low in oxygen. The Chimborazo hillstar, for example, has often been found at over 15,000 feet (4500 m) and breeding within sight of permanent snowfields.

Some species will migrate up and down mountain slopes in search of their food, experiencing great variation in altitude as the seasons change. The Anna's hummingbird, which breeds in the Santa Monica mountains of California, moves in summer to the flower-filled mountain meadows where it can find plenty of food. In winter it moves back down to the chapparal where a species of wild gooseberry (*Ribes*) flowers freely. It is able to breed at this time of year because of the abundance of this important food plant. Similarly, in Costa Rica, four species of hummingbird breed high up the mountains, but only one species, the Fiery-throated hummingbird, remains at high altitudes throughout the year. The Sparkling violet-ear breeds at over 13,000 feet (4000 m) in the mountains of Peru, but in winter it descends to much lower altitudes, where the climate is more agreeable and food is more easily obtained.

Other species of hummingbird cover vast distances from north to south as they move from summer to winter quarters. Species that breed in the far north are faced with journeys of over 2000 miles (3200 km) to reach their wintering quarters in Mexico or Central America. The Rufous hummingbird, measuring only $3\frac{3}{4}$ inches (10 cm) long and weighing about 4 g (only 0.15 oz) breeds as far north as the southern Alaskan coast. At the end of the breeding season, when the days grow shorter and its food supplies dwindle, it flies back south along Canada's west coast, continues down the west coast of the United States, on through Mexico, and down into Central America, where it finally stops for a few months to feed and recuperate. To make this journey once in a lifetime would be incredible enough, but these tiny birds are able to repeat this migration twice a year for the whole of their lives, and some may live for ten years.

The little Calliope hummingbird, North America's smallest bird, measuring only $3\frac{1}{4}$ inches (8 cm) long, also manages this journey twice a year, surviving hazardous weather conditions not only on its long migration to and from its wintering quarters, but also in the hills and canyons where it breeds.

On the east coast of the United States the tiny Ruby-throated hummingbird, which weighs less than 4g and is no more than $3\frac{3}{4}$ inches (10 cm) long, faces a similar marathon at the start and end of its breeding season. Some Ruby-throats breed as far north as Hudson Bay in Canada, and many breed in the northern states of New England. In the course of their arduous journey south these tiny birds are faced with a long sea crossing. The shortest distance across the Gulf of Mexico is about 500 miles (800 km) and this must be crossed non-stop. There is no chance of obtaining nectar for fuel on the journey, so the tiny migrants need to build up their fat reserves by feeding on insects before making the crossing in an amazing non-stop flight. Many must perish in storms, but many more must make the crossing successfully and arrive at the Yucatan peninsula, where they can feed and rest again. Some of the migrants get blown off course by cross-winds and turn up on various Caribbean islands; these are often juvenile birds making their first migration. In the spring the males set off for the breeding grounds first, arriving in the northern states at about the time the cherry trees are in blossom. They may gather in some numbers around the flowers on a tree, creating a distinct buzzing sound, like a swarm of bees, as they fly energetically from flower to flower. The males are always the

The Rufous hummingbird breeds as far north as Alaska and migrates south to Panama for the winter. Castillesa flowers provide it with plenty of nectar.

The Calliope hummingbird is North America's smallest bird, and ranges from British Colombia south to California and Mexico.

first to arrive, and when the females join them their courtship display begins and the breeding season gets into full swing. At the end of the breeding season, at around the time of the first frosts of autumn, the tiny birds, including the newly fledged young, will start to fly south to their winter quarters. Sometimes a sharp overnight frost will chill a bird so much that it will feel quite lifeless when picked up from the ground. Often it can be revived by warming it in the hands, and then, after being fed a solution of honey and sugar, it will be able to fly off again. By the end of September most of them will be well on their way to the tropics.

Costa's hummingbird is a migrant which returns early to its breeding ground.

The tiny Northern parula warbler, which breeds in many of the eastern states of the United States, has been seen alive and well in Great Britain on a number of occasions, having survived an ocean crossing of over 3000 miles (4800 km). At $4\frac{1}{2}$ inches (11 cm) long this little warbler is only a fraction larger than the Ruby-throated hummingbird, yet it is clearly able to store sufficient energy in order to endure this long trip without feeding. The Green-backed firecrown has been seen on the Falkland Islands on very few occasions, although it breeds regularly on the Argentinian coast only 250 miles (400 km) away.

The hummingbirds which live in luxuriant tropical rainforests are largely sedentary; that is, they do not carry out either altitudinal or long distance migrations. Their food is available throughout the year and so there is no need to risk long trips. On the island of Trinidad both the Hairy hermit and Guy's hermit have been marked in attempts to find out more about their movements. It appears that they do not wander at all, being regularly found in the same limited area of forest. The Long-tailed hermit, found in the rainforests of Costa Rica, has the same sedentary nature and rarely leaves its home range.

A few species are nomadic; that is, they wander from one area to another in search of food. These movements are not seasonal and

Apart from the Ruby-throated's appearances on various Caribbean islands during its annual migration, it is very unusual for hummingbirds to make long sea crossings and survive. They differ in this respect from many other small birds such as warblers which regularly turn up as rarities many thousands of miles away from where they originated.

The female Rufous hummingbird lacks the reddish coloration of the male. It migrates one of the longest distances of any hummingbird.

may be quite irregular. The White-eared hummingbird moves to wherever it can find flowers in bloom, abandoning an area quickly if its food supply fails.

EVOLUTION AND THE SPREAD OF HUMMINGBIRDS

There are no fossil records of hummingbirds to give us clues about their early ancestry and origins as their tiny bodies and delicate skeletons are unlikely to leave good imprints. It is only through studies of comparative anatomy that we are able to link them with the swifts. It is highly likely that the hummingbirds arose from some ancestral, swift-like bird living in what is now tropical South America. The hummingbird family shows such great diversity and covers such a vast geographical range that it must have undergone a very long period of adaptive radiation – that is, slowly evolving different body forms, bill shapes, courtship patterns, and migration tendencies to suit a variety of ecological niches. It is thought that this process of evolution began back in the early Tertiary period, about 60 to 70 million years ago.

Although the hummingbirds have been able to colonize a huge area of both North and South America, they have been unable to colonize other continents separated from them by the oceans. No hummingbirds are found in the Old World at all. The only birds that remotely resemble them are the sunbirds of Africa and the Middle East, but these lack

the hovering flight of hummingbirds and differ from them in several other ways.

The early hummingbird ancestors probably resembled the present day hermit hummingbirds but, like the closely related swifts, would have fed exclusively on insects. Some of the insects would probably have been caught as they visited flowers, and this association with flowers could have led to the beginning of the nectar-feeding habit. Gradually, modifications of the bill and the tongue would have made nectar feeding easier. Linked with this, the development of powerful flight muscles and the unique wing and skeletal structure enabled hummingbirds to reach a great variety of flowers unexploited by any other vertebrates.

Hummingbirds have evolved to fill an ecological niche which has not been exploited by any other birds. Their extraordinary flying skills have enabled them to capitalize on the abundant nectar provided by flowers. They compete for this nectar with a few insects, notably bees and moths, but the flowers have evolved too, and they show many adaptations designed to attract hummingbirds but prevent insects from stealing the nectar. In Central America and the south-western United States the Agave, or Century plant, *Agave americana*, produces copious nectar and this is exploited by both hummingbirds and bats, but as the bats feed only at night when the hummingbirds are roosting, there is no real competition. Both bats and hummingbirds manage to pollinate the Agave.

The abundance of nectar-producing flowers, found from ground level to forest canopy height and at altitudes ranging from sea-level to over 15,000 feet (4500 m), has produced a further variety of body sizes, bill shapes, and feeding habits, so within this one family, all members of which share the basic hummingbird characteristics, is an enormous variety which will repay many years of study and reward the patient observer with plenty of delightful memories.

CLASSIFICATION

Hummingbirds belong to the large family of birds known as the non-passerines, or non-perching birds. This family includes birds as different in size and appearance as gamebirds, seabirds, waders, birds of prey, herons and pigeons. The non-passerines can boast both the largest and the smallest members of the bird world; just think of the difference in size between an Ostrich and a Bee hummingbird! The other large bird family, known as the passerines, or perching birds, includes the songbirds, with thrushes, flycatchers, warblers, and swallows among the many familiar groups.

The world's smallest bird is the Bee hummingbird, found on the islands of Cuba and Pinos and nowhere else. Measuring only $2\frac{1}{4}$ inches (6 cm) long, it is smaller than many of the hawk moths and, at less than 2 g, weighs about one twentieth as much as some of the larger beetles. An Ostrich weighs 50,000 times as much as a Bee hummingbird, and some of the largest flying birds, such as swans and bustards, weigh about 8000 times

as much. The Bee hummingbird is not a very common species; an inhabitant of gardens and woods, it is absent from many apparently suitable areas. It both looks and sounds like a bee as it hovers around flowers. Unlike most of the other hummingbirds, which hold their tails level or downwards as they feed at flowers, the Bee hummingbird hovers with its tail cocked up. As it flies rapidly from flower to flower, it utters several high-pitched squeaks and twitters, and it is quite vocal if other hummingbirds of different species are present. Slightly larger, but still an unbelievably small bird at $2\frac{1}{2}$ inches (7 cm) long, is the Vervain hummingbird, named after one of its favorite food plants. It is much more widespread on the islands of Jamaica and Hispaniola.

For a long time hummingbirds were grouped with the swifts, because the two families shared remarkable powers of flight. In fact the internal anatomy of their wings is very similar. Both have greatly reduced 'arm' bones but very flexible shoulder joints and an extended 'hand' which supports the flight feathers. However, although both bird families are extremely skilled at flight, there are important differences in their flying abilities. Hummingbirds do not stay airborne for the prolonged periods that swifts are capable of. The European swift is thought to sleep on the wing and is very rarely seen perching. Hummingbirds, however, spend the night on twigs and often perch for brief periods during the day. They are unable to glide for great distances like the swifts, but they do have great maneuverability in the air, being able to fly sideways, backwards, and even upside down.

Swifts are amongst the dullest of birds, most of them lacking any of the bright colors found in hummingbirds. Both sexes of swifts help at the nest and it is thought that they form strong pair bonds. Hummingbirds on

The beautiful plumage of the Ruby topaz hummingbird attracted bird trappers who caught many of them for export to Europe.

the other hand do not pair and in many cases the males are polygamous; that is, they will mate with more than one female. In most species the males will make no attempt to help with nest building, feeding or raising the young.

For all these reasons hummingbirds have been removed from the order Apodiformes and placed in an order of their own, now known as the Trochiliformes. Out of all the 28 groups of non-passerines the hummingbirds have been placed at the top of the family tree of evolution, as they are thought to represent the highest point of development of all these bird families.

CONSERVATION

Much of the early work on the naming and classifying of hummingbirds was carried out by the so-called cabinet ornithologists of European museums and universities, who never saw the birds in their natural habitats at all. Instead they studied specimens brought to Europe for the purpose of being turned into costume jewelry or to adorn ladies hats. Vast numbers of hummingbirds were trapped or shot, and their dried skins were packed into crates to be shipped across the Atlantic. The traders sometimes allowed ornithologists access to their imports before they were turned into ornaments, and many new species

The dazzling yellow gorget of the Ruby topaz hummingbird does not show its bright coloration when seen from the side.

were described from their dried skins alone. There were very few records to accompany these specimens, and in most cases the best that was known about them was the country of origin. There was no idea of the habitat they were caught in or the range they covered. It was naturally the most brilliantly colored specimens that were prized by the collectors, so the early records show a preponderance of males of these species and little evidence of females or the less conspicuous species of hermit hummingbirds.

There are records of a London dealer importing over 400,000 dead hummingbirds from the West Indies in a single year in the late nineteenth century. Countless millions of hummingbirds must have been slaughtered to satisfy the vanity and curiosity of people who would never know the delight of watching them in the wild. Many of the newly described species of hummingbirds were named after members of European aristocratic families; often the birds have outlived the nobility they were named after.

Our knowledge of hummingbirds is improving all the time, but, sadly, what we are learning is that some species are declining rapidly. New species are discovered from time to time, and they are often found to have very restricted ranges, sometimes being linked to a single remote upland valley. In the 1970s, a previously unrecorded species of sunangel, *Heliangelis regalis*, was discovered in northern Peru, and an unknown metaltail, *Metallura odomae*, was found high up in a Peruvian forest. Some species, known only from their dried skins collected for the European millinery trade in the nineteenth century, have yet to be discovered living in a natural state in the wild. We may never know how many species have already become extinct through overzealous collecting or the destruction of their habitats.

The early collectors certainly took their toll of hummingbirds, and must have seriously depleted some populations by relentless trapping, but at least they left the habitat largely intact, giving an opportunity for the remainder of the population to restore the numbers to their original level. What is happening now is far more serious. We are destroying vast areas of the very habitat which the hummingbirds need in order to survive. Laws that are designed to protect the hummingbirds from trapping and strict controls on exporting and importing live and endangered species are vitally important, but they are meaningless if the birds are left with nowhere to live. A species like the Brown violet-ear is never very common, but it does have a wide geographical range, so the destruction of an isolated area of forest will not seriously reduce its numbers. Rarer species, however, with much more restricted ranges, such as the Marvellous spatuletail, could be wiped out forever if their limited areas of forest are destroyed. Hummingbirds and their flowers have evolved together, so wiping out one will effectively destroy the other.

The White-necked jacobin is a widespread and common tropical species seen by many of the early explorers in South America.

CHAPTER 2

COLOR AND FORM

Colors and iridescence

Feather structure and arrangement

Differences between the sexes

Subdued colors

The Red-tailed comet has a brilliantly colored rump and tail, but lacks bright colors under the chin.

Colors and iridescence

Reading through a list of hummingbird's names is like reading a jeweller's catalogue. Many precious stones are involved, with their names including sapphire, ruby, topaz, emerald, beryl, lazuli, jewel, tourmaline, and gem, and they are further embellished with adjectives like glittering, brilliant, magnificent, sparkling, shining, spangled, fiery, and gilded. Several shining metals are used to add lustre to what are already exciting names: bronze, steel, copper, and gold are all included to help increase the impression of bright and iridescent plumage.

Names reminiscent of a display in a jeweller's window imply that the bearers will be equally glittering. How many people have been surprised or even disappointed by their first glimpse of the Ruby-throated hummingbird when, expecting to see a deep ruby-red throat, they have instead seen something looking quite dull and ordinary? Watching the bird while it is still, or perhaps only viewing it from the side, gives a poor idea of

When seen from the wrong angle the gorget of the male Ruby-throated hummingbird does not look red.

the splendors it can reveal. If it turns its head quickly it may then show how its name was earned, for that same throat which looked so dull in one light suddenly flashes with fire and is really ruby colored. In many species of hummingbirds the males have a patch of brilliant color which flashes and burns with light and then quickly becomes subdued again. Often the patches are found on the throat, where they are known as gorgets, but some hummingbirds have equally brilliant markings on their heads, backs, or flanks.

The brilliant colors produced by hummingbirds are not true colors. They are the result of the reflection of light rays rather than of pigmentation. The bright colors of birds such as cardinals, crossbills, and the Rufous-sided towhee are produced by pigmentation in the feathers. Reds, blacks, browns, yellows, and other shades in between are produced when the pigments absorb some of the wavelengths that make up white light and reflect others in all directions. Whatever the angle of viewing, the color does not change.

Structural colors are produced when light is reflected in a certain way from the surface of a colorless body. If a few drops of oil are spilled onto a puddle in the road a beautiful array of colors will be formed. Similarly, the thinnest film of liquid forming the skin of a soap bubble will reflect the light and produce colors across the whole range of the spectrum. This is very similar to the way in which the feathers of the hummingbird produce its beautiful iridescent coloring. The surfaces of some of its feathers are modified in such a way as to produce the dazzling effect. When white

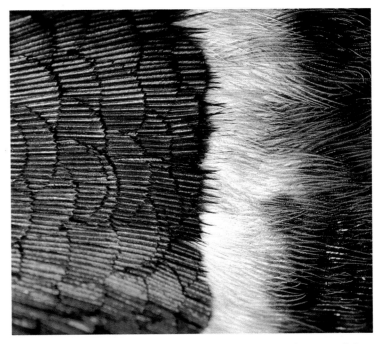

The brilliant colors, shown in close-up in the gorget feathers of this Sunstar, are a result of the reflection of light rather than pigmentation of the feathers.

light is split up and the various wavelengths are scattered in several different directions, then a variety of colors will be seen. The blue sky, a rainbow, and a blazing red sunset can all be explained in this way. These effects are produced by minute particles of various materials in the atmosphere; they may be caused by tiny droplets of water, or by dust from a volcanic eruption.

On a hummingbird's feathers there are many minute lens-shaped structures arranged in a mosaic-like pattern. Microscopical examination of these structures, initially by

Crawford Greenewalt, revealed that they are made up of an arrangement of even smaller platelets, in each of which are minute air bubbles. The result is that when light waves hit these structures they are both refracted, that is, their frequency is altered, and reflected back towards the source. Variations in the thickness of the platelets and the size and number of the air bubbles causes differences in the structural colors produced. The angle from which the observer views the hummingbird determines the color seen, so the glittering gorget of a male hummingbird may change from a shimmering red or purple

to a much more dull green or black. All the iridescent colors of hummingbirds are produced by interference, but the rest of their body coloration is produced in the more normal way, by pigmentation. Lacking the light-reflecting platelets, the feathers on the back of a hummingbird reflect the light equally in all directions, and so from whatever angle they are viewed they will always appear to be green, brown, rufous, or a deep indigo-black.

FEATHER STRUCTURE AND ARRANGEMENT

The feathers are remarkable structures even without their extraordinary light-reflecting qualities. They must serve to keep the hummingbird warm, act as some sort of camouflage when it is roosting and provide the means of flight. Three types of feathers are found on the body, but they all conform to the same basic plan. The shaft of the feather is rooted in a follicle in the skin, out of which come the barbs. These interlock to form the blade of the feather, each barb being provided with many microscopic barbules; on these are found the still smaller barbicels, tiny hooks that link up with each other. The barbules of the neck feathers, for example, contain the light-reflecting platelets. The flight feathers in the wing have a stronger and much longer

Occasionally albino hummingbirds are found, such as this unusual Ruby-throated, seen at a garden-feeder in Ohio. A few white feathers on a bird are common, but total albinism is rare.

The Giant hummingbird is the size of a Starling. It lacks the brilliant colors seen in many other hummingbirds.

The striking gorget of the male Blue-throated hummingbird flashes in the sunlight as it approaches a flower to feed.

shaft than the other feathers, and the barbs are also much longer, giving a greater surface area to each feather. Body feathers have a shorter and more curved shaft. These comprise the bulk of the feathers on a bird's body and form the main insulating layer. Beneath them would normally lie the soft down feathers with their more delicate shaft and softer barbules, which make them feel

The male Allen's hummingbird has a magnificent glossy gorget which flashes an orange-red color when turned in the light.

more 'feathery'. These serve only to insulate the body and, although they are very important for birds that live in colder regions and need good insulation, they are largely absent in most species of hummingbirds. In order to maintain a high body temperature when the surrounding air temperature drops, hummingbirds have to produce more heat by increasing their rate of metabolism; in most other birds it would be possible to increase the

insulating properties of the feathers by ruffling them up to trap more air. Hummingbirds only ruffle up their feathers when they want to lose heat prior to becoming torpid, as this process actually exposes the skin to the air and hastens heat loss.

The Ruby-throated hummingbird, typical of the rest of its family, has about 950 feathers on its body, the lowest number recorded for any bird species. The Whistling swan has over 25,000 body feathers, and even the tiny Least sandpiper can boast a body covering of nearly 4500 feathers. The comparatively low number quite adequately covers the hummingbird's much smaller body, however, and it suffers no ill effects as a result. Despite their low number the feathers are quite densely distributed on the body, particularly around the head and neck.

The streamlined shape of some species of hummingbirds is modified to provide structures used in display by the males during courtship. Several species have feathers that can be extended from the throat to form a ruff which, when combined with a dazzling iridescence and a lively flight pattern, makes a very eye-catching display. A few species have crests that can be raised and serve the same function as the ruffs. The Horned sungem, from Brazil, has a broad forked crest, while the Black-breasted plovercrest, from south Brazil, Paraguay and Argentina, has a magnificent crest which is longer than its bill.

This male Calliope hummingbird has distended its bib feathers whilst feeding. They are also distended during its courtship display.

The male Streamer-tail hummingbird has a deeply forked tail which is important in its courtship display; it produces a whirring sound as the bird accelerates in flight.

In a few species the tail has become greatly extended for no other reason than to accentuate the male's courtship display. Certainly, the enormously long forked tail of the male Violet-tailed sylph, or the scissor-like crossed-over tail of the Crimson topaz, can have very little beneficial effect on flight. Residents of Jamaica call the Green-and-black streamertail, the 'doctor bird'. It is a common and widespread bird on the island and earned its name, supposedly, from its black head, which bears a fanciful resemblance to the top hats that doctors used to wear. As it flies, the

The male Frilled coquette is a very showy hummingbird which has a striking brown crest. It can also extend the brightly colored bib feathers.

streamertail produces a humming sound, but this is the result not of the whirring of its wings but of the air rushing past the long tail streamers. In many species the tail feathers, or at least one or two pairs of them, are modified further by being narrower or notched at the tip to produce the whistling or whirring sounds heard as the bird flies.

Many of the names of hummingbirds hint at the structure of the plumage: long-tailed, broad-tailed, streamertail, wedge-tailed, and scissor-tailed all conjur up pictures of the bird's tail, while sabrewing, puffleg, and helmetcrest tell us something more about other parts of the body.

Long-tailed hummingbirds are abundant in South America and many of them have strikingly beautiful colors to match. They inhabit open glades and woodland edges where their display flights are seen to best advantage by the females. The Marvellous spatuletail, or Loddiges' racket-tail, has one of the most extraordinary tails of all. Its two outermost tail feathers are completely lacking in barbules except at the tip, where there is a broad, purplish-black blade. The wire-like shafts cross over behind the bird, and as it flies the broad tips of the feathers look like tiny outriders flying along behind it. The next pair of feathers is more conventional in structure, but they are still very long and do not cross over. This is a rare and little known species; it has been infrequently observed in the wild because of its scarcity and the remoteness of its breeding sites. It was first recorded in the 1840s from a single skin which was acquired for the European costume jewelry and millinery trade. No one discovered its breeding site until professional rather than the usual native collectors visited a small and remote valley about 9000 feet (2750 m) up in the Peruvian Andes. A few more specimens were collected, but because of the remoteness of its mountainous habitat little is known, even today, of its life history.

The Frilled coquette has a superb chestnut crest and an iridescent green throat and forehead. Its body is a rich deep brown, the perfect background for the crest and gorget. This tiny hummingbird, no longer than $2\frac{1}{2}$ inches (7 cm), performs a very attractive display dance. It swoops and dives as if it is on the end of an imaginary pendulum, making bee-like buzzing sounds as it does so. The male performs this dance in front of the female, reaching the lowest point of the swing immediately in front of her; at this point the buzzing is also at its most intense. This attractive little bird inhabits tropical forests in central and southern Brazil, and despite its very small size it will defend an area of food plants quite aggressively; because of this behavior it is often the only species of hummingbird to be present in some areas.

The pufflegs are a family of hummingbirds having many long, fluffy feathers on their legs which form powder-puffs around their feet. They are usually paler in color than the rest of the plumage. These birds are fairly widespread in equatorial South America, being found in Ecuador and western Venezuela. The Glowing puffleg is a popular bird in captivity, and many have been collected from the wild. Some of the pufflegs are on the International Council for Bird Protection (ICBP) world checklist of threatened birds, partly because of over-collecting, but mainly because of destruction of their habitat. The Turquoise-throated puffleg was first identified from dead birds exported to Europe but has not been seen in recent years in its former haunts in Ecuador and Colombia. Both the Colorful puffleg and the Black-thighed puffleg are reduced to small and isolated populations, and the Hoary puffleg is now becoming scarce; it was formerly exported to European aviculturists in large numbers.

DIFFERENCES BETWEEN THE SEXES

Most hummingbirds exhibit a very strong sexual dimorphism; that is, there are very great differences in the appearance of the sexes. There may be size differences, but more typically there will be differences in the amount of iridescence of the gorgets, in the presence of tail streamers or crests, or in the basic body color. It is almost always the males who are larger or who show the greatest degree of coloration or modification to the plumage. In some species the sexes are so completely different that for many years ornithologists thought they were looking at separate species. There are other species, however, where the sex differences are not very marked, and in some closely related species, such as the Ruby-throated and Black-chinned, it is almost impossible to distinguish between females and juveniles in the field.

The female Purple-crowned fairy is unusual among hummingbirds in that she has a much longer tail than the male. Her tail can be an inch (2.5 cm) longer than the male's tail, although the coloring is very similar. The females are a beautiful iridescent green with pure white undersides. White is an unusual color in hummingbirds and when present is normally only seen in very small patches, such as in the tiny 'ears' of some species. The Purple-crowned fairies inhabit the upper tree canopy of tropical forests, occurring up to 5000 feet (1500 m) above sea level in Brazil and Central America. The white undersides may be an effective form of disruptive camouflage, as any predator looking upwards towards the tree canopy will see bright patches of light between the leaves. The white undersides of the hummingbirds will then be very difficult to pick out against the sky. Similarly, a predator such as a hawk looking down onto the canopy from above will see only green leaves, and the green backs of the Purple-crowned fairies will be equally difficult to pick out from that angle. Purple-crowned fairies do occasionally venture down to the lower levels of the forest in order to collect nectar if none is available in the canopy layer. They will sometimes be tempted down by squeaking sounds. A birdwatcher who is adept at using a bird-caller or who can produce convincing squeaks with a blade of grass or by sucking the back of his hand may get good results in this way.

The female Black-chinned hummingbird lacks the male's black gorget.

White is an unusual color in hummingbirds; it may serve to make this White-chested emerald more difficult to see against the broken light of the tree canopy.

SUBDUED COLORS

Not all species of hummingbirds are dazzling and conspicuous. In habitats where there is little sunshine to reflect from the feathers and set them glowing, the males as well as the females have much more subdued coloration. The hermit hummingbirds are a large group which lives in forests where little sunlight penetrates the canopy. They mostly have long bills, and their colors are a subtle mixture of bronze, green, brown, and cinnamon, which blend well with the dappled light of the forest floor. A few males have white inner-tail feathers which are visible when they flick their tails up and down while singing. The largest hummingbird of all, the starling-sized Giant hummingbird, from the southern part of the Andes, is also one of the dullest, with a fairly uniform drab brown plumage, brightened only by the rich cinnamon coloration on its throat and chest. It has no shining gorget and lacks any form of crest or tail streamer to add interest to its plumage. In good light there is a purplish sheen to its wings, and the under-tail feathers are white. The sexes are almost exactly alike, females normally only being distinguishable by their nesting behavior. The Giant hummingbird has been found living at over 14,000 feet (4250 m) up in the Andes, and its large size is probably advantageous in helping it to maintain its normally high body temperature at that altitude.

The subtle colors of the Hermit hummingbirds make them inconspicuous in their rainforest habitat. This Hermit is sheltering beneath a leaf during a tropical rain-storm.

The Green hermit has white outer-tail feathers which are used in its tail-bobbing courtship display.

CHAPTER 3

FLIGHT

Flying skills

Speed of flight

Wing and muscle structure

Rate of wingbeats

The hummingbird's metabolism

By hovering, the Black-chinned hummingbird can obtain nectar from flowers which are out of reach of most insects.

High-speed flash photography has been used to freeze the movement of the wings of this Broad-billed hummingbird. As the Broad-billed hummingbird comes to a stop in mid-air, the wings are brought forward and the tail is lowered.

FLYING SKILLS

One of the many striking features about hummingbirds is the way they fly with such apparent ease. Hovering is accomplished on almost invisible wings, and twists, turns, swoops, and dives are all performed with what appears to be very little effort. Much of the time this activity is accompanied by the characteristic humming sounds. The bird often appears to be floating, and from a fixed position it can dart away, stopping as suddenly as it started, and just as easily turn to face in a totally different direction. Hummingbirds will often dart out of the undergrowth to hover in front of the face of a human intruder and, once curiosity has been satisfied, will dart away again and remain hidden from view. No matter how awkward the angle of a flower, even if it hangs straight downwards, or how well concealed under a leaf an insect may be, the hummingbird will be able to reach it.

The flight of the hummingbird is often described as being rather like that of a helicopter; it too can hover, change direction and fly rapidly forwards. What the helicopter cannot do, however, is fly backwards, turn and fly upside down, or suddenly stop dead in mid-air, especially at the end of a rapid nose-dive. The whirling rotors of a helicopter provide lift and propulsion, but a tail rotor is needed to stop the helicopter from rotating, whereas in the hummingbird the wings do all the work, providing lift, propulsion, and the means of changing direction, accelerating or braking.

Watching a hummingbird flitting from flower to flower or moving effortlessly between leaves and twigs is rather like watching a fish swimming; the bird seems to be buoyant in the air in the same way that a fish is buoyant in water. It is able to hover with its body in the horizontal position when feeding from a flower with a horizontal nectar tube, or hold its body in a near vertical position when visiting a flower that hangs downwards like a fuchsia or columbine. With its body held motionless in the air its bill can be moved skilfully into position so that it can reach into flowers above, below, and on its own level. Having finished feeding it can then withdraw its bill from the flower, fly backwards for a short distance, swivel round on a fixed point and dart off to investigate another source of food.

While flying rapidly forward a hummingbird can make a sudden nose-dive, hurtling downwards at an incredible speed, only to stop about two inches (5 cm) from the ground and shoot off in a quite different direction at the same incredible speed. When leaving her nest the female hummingbird often can be seen to fly backwards before turning round and darting off at the same speed. If confronted by a predator in a confined space the hummingbird can do an amazing maneuver. It can perform an instant back somersault and fly off upside down for a few inches before regaining its normal upright position and flying away unharmed. This is an effective way of momentarily startling a predator and leaving just enough time to make a speedy escape.

When hovering in front of a flower and about to feed, the body of the Blue-throated hummingbird is held vertically while the wings beat backwards and forward.

SPEED OF FLIGHT

Although the hummingbird seems to dart everywhere at the same rapid rate it is capable of varying its speed as appropriate to its needs. Flitting from flower to flower, for example, does not require the same great speed which is needed when escaping from a predatory bird or when pursuing an equally agile insect.

Experimental work has shown that the hummingbird can increase or decrease its speed quite easily. It is only possible to measure its speed of flight accurately by placing a captive hummingbird in a wind tunnel. The bird's favorite food is placed at one end of the tunnel, usually in the form of a nectar feeder, and the bird is placed in the tunnel as the air current is switched on. If the bird is able to make headway against the wind it must be flying faster than the wind speed

indicated. The point at which the bird can no longer move forward and starts to get blown backwards indicates its maximum forward speed. Speeds of up to 60 miles per hour (95 km/h) have been claimed for the Ruby-throat by observers who have paced it in forward flight from their cars. A drag effect may be influencing the speed here; so far, the wind tunnel studies have shown that a top speed of less than half that is more likely. However, it should be remembered that in laboratory conditions the bird may not be as

With the body held vertically the Blue-throated hummingbird can easily insert its bill into a corolla tube.

relaxed as it might be in the wild and so may not reach its true maximum speed. Some observers have timed hummingbirds flying over marked out courses using a stopwatch, but again there are difficulties here as the bird does not always fly in a straight line, and it sometimes accelerates and then slows down during the space of a short flight.

Unlike most other birds, the hummingbird is flying at full speed almost as soon as it has left its perch. It starts to beat its wings before it leaves its resting place; sometimes a tiny twig is lifted gently just before the bird lets go with its feet and leaves its perch. Another unique feature of the hummingbird in flight is that it does not need to use its legs to give it an extra spring into the air. When arriving at a perch the hummingbird does not need to slow down before landing; its co-ordination is so good that it can stop and land instantly in a way that would be highly dangerous for a large bird like a swan or eagle. Stroboscopic studies of the Broad-tailed hummingbird have shown that take-off is accomplished in only 7/100ths of a second. A stroboscope is a device that can produce rapid pulses of light. If the pulses of light synchronize exactly with the rate of wingbeats of the bird, the wings will always be illuminated at the same point in their up-and-down cycle, and the bird will appear to be hovering on motionless outstretched wings. The rate of light pulses can be read from the stroboscope controls, and this will indicate the bird's wingbeats per second.

The Lucifer hummingbird breeds in Mexico, where it is quite common, and just a few breed in the Chisos Mountains of Texas. This is a species sometimes kept in bird collections, and one individual in a European Zoo was seen by its keeper to hover continuously for four hours. Its rate of wingbeats has been estimated to be 75 per second, so in that four-hour period it must have flapped its wings over one million times. A further feat achieved by the Lucifer hummingbird is to shatter a plate-glass window. A loosely fitting pane of glass in an aviary vibrated at exactly the same frequency as the bird's rapidly beating wings, and when this was maintained for more than a few seconds the result was the shattering of the glass into tiny pieces.

The supposed rapid flight of a tiny bird is in reality an optical illusion. The average hummingbird does not fly as fast as many larger birds. The wind-tunnel studies indicate a maximum forward flight speed of about 25 miles per hour (40 km/h) for most species, although when the bird is plummeting downwards, as in the display flight of the Allen's hummingbird, it can reach speeds of nearly 60 miles per hour (95 km/h). This makes its ability to brake suddenly only a matter of a few inches from the ground all the more remarkable. Studies of hummingbirds flying over measured distances while being timed with a stopwatch have indicated speeds varying from 14 to 47 miles per hour (23 to 75 km/h). An average speed of 25 miles per hour (40 km/h) for most hummingbirds may not seem very impressive, but if you remember that thrushes and pigeons, birds of far greater size, fly at speeds also averaging about this, you will then be more impressed by the speed of such tiny birds.

The short, rounded wings do have one shortcoming, however. They are quite unsuitable for soaring or gliding flight. Hummingbirds are not able to utilize thermals or updrafts from rock faces in the way that some seabirds or birds of prey can. When the hummingbird is airborne, it has to use its wings and expend energy almost the entire time. When flying foward in normal flight the wings are rested momentarily, and the bird glides forward for a short distance before a further burst of rapid wingbeats commences. This sequence of a series of rapid wingbeats followed by the briefest of pauses and then more wingbeats seems to allow just enough time to rest the muscles during periods of sustained activity. It helps explain how the hummingbird copes so well with flying over great distances and keeping airborne for hours on end as, for example, when it is undertaking its annual migration.

Observations of birds in aviaries have shown that they spend very little time perching, especially during the day, and those species which migrate are clearly able to cover great distances over the sea, when there is no opportunity at all for resting. Being unable to glide or soar over long distances they must maintain their rapid cycles of wingbeats for hours at a time. Hummingbirds do perch from time to time when they are feeding, although normally the arrangement of the flowers means that perching is not possible. The Tyrian metaltail, a bird of open habitats in high mountain regions will often cling to a flower to feed rather than hover in front of it. The low oxygen levels at high altitudes make hovering hard work, so any saving like this will help conserve valuable energy.

WING AND MUSCLE STRUCTURE

The secret to the hummingbird's great agility and maneuverability in the air lies in the special adaptations of its skeleton and muscles. The wing of a bird is the limb which corresponds to the human arm; the bones and muscles are modified to support the flight feathers and make powerful downbeats. In the hummingbird the normal wing pattern for a bird is modified still further. Imagine a human arm in which the long bones have been shortened to about one quarter of their normal length. Then visualize the bones of the hand stretched out to form an elongated structure which supports the feathers. At the top of the arm the shoulder joint is very flexible in humans, allowing movement in almost a complete circle; the hummingbird has even greater flexibility here and, although the wrist and elbow joints are fairly rigid, the whole wing can be moved through about 180 degrees. The combination of the reduced skeleton and a highly flexible shoulder joint allows the hummingbird's wing to make movements in almost any direction. The wing can be rotated so that the front or

The extended wing of the White-necked jacobin shows the elongated primary flight feathers and the smaller number of secondary feathers.

leading edge is pointing forward on both the upbeat and the downbeat. In all other birds it is only the downbeat which provides power and therefore lift. When the wing of a bird like a pigeon is being returned to the position above the body ready for the next downbeat, it does not provide any lift; it has to be moved upwards in such a way that it does not cause any drag or backwards movement. The wing is normally folded at the wrist and elbow joints, and the primaries are splayed out to reduce resistance to the air. By turning its wing forward the hummingbird is able to provide power as the wing returns to its starting position above the body.

The arrangement of the feathers on the hummingbird's wing differs from that of most other species in the number of primary and secondary flight feathers present. The primaries are the long feathers at the tip of the wing which provide the greatest surface area. Hummingbirds have ten of these feathers, whereas in many passerine species one of the primaries is very much reduced, and effectively they have only nine. The secondary feathers are positioned between the primaries and the bird's body. In broad-winged species, such as buzzards or vultures, there may be as many as 40 secondaries, but in the hummingbird, which has much shorter, rounded wings, there are only six or seven.

High-speed photography has enabled us to study the movements made by the wings as the hummingbird hovers. In normal hovering flight the wings describe a shallow figure of eight, moving backwards and forward, instead of up and down as in a normal bird's flight, and in some species the tail may be splayed out to provide further stability. When flying forward the wings beat up and down, and in backwards flight they are rotated behind the body.

Braking suddenly in mid-air is achieved by putting the wings into reverse action, splaying the tail feathers outwards and drawing the head in. This has the effect of arresting even the most rapid forward flight, enabling the bird to stop just short of an obstacle or quickly change direction if alarmed. Large birds are quite unable to do this; they would lose their balance rapidly if they tried instant braking or mid-air turns. An eagle needs several yards of open space in which to slow down, and a swan or a goose would require a long stretch of open water to slow its descent safely.

RATE OF WINGBEATS

On average the hummingbird's wings make about 24 beats per second, each beat being counted as one complete up and down movement. Large hummingbirds, such as the Giant, make only about seven or eight beats per second, whereas some insects, such as mosquitoes, make about 500 beats per second. It was thought at one time that hummingbirds had the fastest rate of wingbeats of any bird, but careful studies using stroboscopes have shown that some species, such as chickadees, make even more rapid wingbeats, perhaps as many as 30–40 beats per second in normal flight. This may seem surprising, but it should be remembered that the hummingbird is able to utilize both the upbeat and downbeat, whereas other small birds can gain lift only from the downbeat; their wings therefore have to work much harder in order to provide the same amount of lift. A flying swan beats it wings slowly enough for us to be able to follow the movements with our eyes. A rate of about 1½ beats per second is normal for a swan in flight.

There are occasions when the hummingbird does make such rapid wingbeats that even high-speed photography is unable to freeze the movement. Very windy conditions or the need to evade a predator may lead to a rate of around 170 beats per second; it is unlikely that this rate can be sustained for long, but it certainly is an effective way of escaping instantly! The courtship displays of some species, such as the Rufous and Ruby-throated, also involve rapid flights and aerial displays, and then the rate of wingbeats can rise as high as a staggering 200 beats per second. Observations of the Broad-tailed hummingbird have shown that in normal hovering flight it makes about 55 wingbeats per second. This is not fast enough to produce any humming sounds, but as the rate of wingbeats rises to 75 beats per second, such as when the bird moves off in forward flight, the humming sound begins and it can be heard quite clearly. The male Broad-tailed has a spectacular courtship flight in which he swings up and down in front of the female describing U-shaped arcs in the air. To achieve this his wings are moved at a rate of at least 200 beats per second, and the humming

sound is much louder as the air whistles between the narrow tips of his primary flight feathers.

The slow rate of seven or eight wingbeats per second of the Giant hummingbird gives it a rather different appearance in flight from most other hummingbirds; if it flies across in front of an observer it has a curious swooping, undulating flight pattern, with its wingbeats occurring in bursts with brief pauses in between. It looks rather like a woodpecker in flight and is often difficult to spot as it spends relatively more time perching than do most other hummingbirds. Despite its larger size and its slower wingbeats the Giant hummingbird is still capable of hovering, flying backwards, and performing many of the other feats carried out by much smaller hummingbirds.

In most birds the depressor muscles, which provide the muscular power for the wing's downbeat, are considerably larger than the elevator muscles, which are used to raise the wings above the body; only in the hummingbirds are the elevator muscles almost half as big as the depressor muscles. Other birds have elevator muscles that are only about 5–10 per cent of the weight of the depressors. The American robin, a bird which does not hover but does carry out long migrations, has depressor muscles that make up about 14 per cent of its body weight, but its elevator muscles are much smaller and make up only about 2 per cent of the bird's body weight. A further adaptation is seen in the sternum, or breast bone, which is very prominent in hummingbirds, providing a firm attachment for these very large flight muscles. As a proportion of the total body weight the flight muscles make up about 35–40 per cent – considerably more than in a similar small bird, such as a chickadee. The large bones and the flight muscles are positioned in such a way that weight is concentrated near the base of the wing; this contributes to its maneuverability and makes it much easier for the hummingbird to twist and turn in flight and to negotiate small openings and gaps in vegetation.

THE HUMMINGBIRD'S METABOLISM

The hummingbird's heart is, relative to the size of the bird, one of the largest in the animal kingdom. It has a tremendous amount of work to do when the hummingbird is in full flight, and it pumps at a rate of about 21 beats per second. Compare this with the rate of just over one beat per second for the human heart. The rapid conversion of glucose to energy for the flight muscles requires this phenomenal rate of activity. The rate of breathing and uptake of oxygen are both correspondingly high and give the hummingbird one of the highest rates of metabolism in the animal kingdom. The red corpuscles are the cells that give the blood its red color; their function is to carry oxygen. In hummingbirds they are extremely numerous, with far more to the mililiter of blood than in other vertebrates. They are also much smaller, thus giving them a larger surface area for the absorption of oxygen. In order to get this oxygen into its lungs the hummingbird takes about 250 breaths per minute—a far greater rate than the 16 or so to the minute in the resting human. During torpidity all these body functions slow down, and the hummingbird's heart will beat at a much slower rate of 50 to 180 beats per minute. Even this is much higher than the rate for a hibernating small mammal, such as a bat.

In the very small hummingbirds, such as the diminutive Bee hummingbird of Cuba, the wings are relatively short in proportion to the rest of the body, with the primary flight feathers not exceeding the length of the body when fully extended. In larger species, however, such as the White-throated hummingbird, the long wing feathers may extend beyond the body by 25–30 per cent. The very tiny hummingbirds can zoom over long distances like a bullet, keeping on an exactly straight course and arriving dead on target. The wings vibrate so rapidly that they become an indistinct blur, thus increasing the illusion of a bullet whistling past the observer.

The short legs and tiny feet of hummingbirds are of very little use on the ground. Hummingbirds rarely walk or hop and look very distressed and awkward if they are grounded. Their feet are very suitable for grasping thin twigs but no good on flat surfaces. If the hummingbird wants to move a couple of inches along its perch it will fly rather than walk or hop.

A feeding Rufous-tailed hummingbird shows the tiny feet typical of all hummingbirds.

CHAPTER 4

FEEDING

Ruby-throated hummingbirds can be attracted to a variety of nectar-producing garden flowers, especially red ones.

APPETITE

It would seem likely that the smallest warm-blooded vertebrates in the animal kingdom would have small appetites to match their size. The actual amounts of food consumed by a small hummingbird such as the Black-

Garden nectar feeders often attract many birds to feed at the same time. Six Rufous hummingbirds are interested in this feeder.

chinned, as it sips nectar delicately from flowers or picks tiny insects from the air, are indeed very small, but when these tiny quantities are expressed as a proportion of the bird's body weight it is obvious that hummingbirds have enormous appetites.

Some of the earliest studies on the amounts of food consumed by hummingbirds were actually rather misleading, although the investigators were working along the right lines. Hummingbirds visiting gardens were offered sugar or honey solutions in feeding bottles and, after they had finished drinking, the amount they had imbibed was calculated by working out how much was left. In order to compare how much more this volume of food weighed than the bird itself the body of a dead hummingbird was weighed.

Unfortunately, in one investigation carried out in Iowa in 1907 by Miss Althea R. Sherman, the bird she weighed had been dead for some time, and so its weight was significantly less than that of a living bird of the same species. This gave the impression that the bird was actually consuming a quantity of nectar three times greater than the bird's own body weight. In fact, the weight of sugar consumed was probably only about one half of the bird's body weight as the weight of water was not included in the calculations. Miss Sherman was studying free-living Ruby-throated hummingbirds, and she assumed that all males weighed 2.1 g, like the corpse she had obtained. She did not take into consideration how long the bird had been dead and by how much it had dehydrated. In fact, a normal adult Ruby-throat weighs between 2.9 and 3.5 g. This can increase by as much as 50 per cent immediately prior to the long sea crossing of the Gulf of Mexico, when fat reserves are accumulated to act as an energy supply for the non-stop 500 mile (800 km) sea crossing. The decreasing day-length of the end of summer stimulates the hummingbird's endocrine system to produce a hormone that causes this build-up of subcutaneous fat. Non-migratory species lack the high levels of this hormone, and so they do not normally store fat under the skin.

The concentration of the sugar solution was not noted in the early investigations so this too may have led to the impression that the bird was apparently consuming a great deal of food. Also, the investigations were carried out on birds living freely in the wild; they may have been imbibing nectar or other liquids from more natural sources when they were not present at the garden feeder. No account was taken either of the insects eaten by the hummingbirds in addition to the nectar.

Even with our more accurate knowledge we can see that the amounts of food consumed are still very great. If a man ate the same proportion of food each day he would have to eat a pile of glucose weighing about 100 pounds (45 kg); in terms of other foods the quantities needed to yield the same amount of energy would rise to about 150 pounds (68 kg) of bread or several sacks of potatoes weighing about 380 pounds (172 kg)! The average daily consumption of food for an adult male is about $2\frac{1}{2}$ pounds (1.1 kg) of all foods.

THE DAILY DIET

The tiny body of a hummingbird has a very large surface area in proportion to its mass. The bulkier an animal's body, the more heat-producing tissue it has to each square inch of body surface. It is through the body surface that heat is lost to the air, and even though hummingbirds have an insulating covering of feathers they do lose body heat quickly through their relatively large surface area. In order to maintain a high body temperature foods rich in energy must be utilized in the tissues. Sugars are very rich in energy and are quickly oxidized to release it. When taken in the form of nectar from flowers, sugars pass rapidly through the digestive system into the blood stream and then to the body tissues. About 20 minutes after a meal has been consumed it will have passed through the hummingbird's intestines and into the blood stream, where it will then be available for use by the muscles as an energy source.

Frequent visits to flowers rich in nectar will provide the fuel the hummingbird requires to maintain its high body temperature and give it the energy it needs for its powerful flight muscles to function efficiently. During the course of a normal day a hummingbird will visit between 1000 and 2000 flowers. Some flowers release their nectar gradually and will receive many visits, while others may be visited once only. Some flowers are able to control the release of nectar and make it available only at dusk when hummingbirds are anxious to feed before going to roost. This ensures that insects will not be able to steal the nectar as they will mostly have finished flying by then. Similarly, other flowers release nectar only at dawn, when hummingbirds are again very hungry but most insects are not yet on the wing.

Energy-rich foods such as nectar are essential for the hummingbird to maintain its high body temperature. A human has a body temperature of 98.4°F (37.6°C) but the hummingbird's body temperature is a few degrees higher at 102°F (38.5°C). Muscular activity provides heat and so during periods of rapid flight the body is easily kept warm. There is, however, a problem in maintaining this high temperature at night when the bird is perching. Most hummingbirds are known to feed just before going to roost at dusk so that their bodies have sufficient reserves to keep them going through the night, and they are also seen to engage in frenzied bouts of feeding early in the morning to restore the fuel reserves used up during the night. However, in order to survive a long night most hummingbirds will enter a state of torpidity, in which their body temperatures drop to within a few degrees of that of their surroundings. Their rates of respiration and heart beat also drop and they remain in this state until morning.

During periods of torpidity the birds sometimes appear to be dead; they can be handled freely and will not respond to sound or touch. Gentle warming with the hands will eventually bring the birds out of torpor but this may take as long as half an hour. Birds removed from their perches while torpid cannot be placed back on them again, because

their feet will not grip properly. Before entering this state some species of hummingbird have been seen to ruffle their feathers and expose their skin to the air, presumably in an attempt to dissipate body heat more rapidly and hasten their descent into torpor. This apparent waste of hard-earned body heat must be seen as a saving, because when the bird is torpid its demand for energy is very low; it is able to spend long periods in this condition without the need for constant forays in search of food. As long as it has found a safe roosting place out of the reach of predators and harsh weather conditions, it is far more economical to remain in this almost lifeless state despite the possible dangers of being unable to respond to changes in its surroundings.

INSECT FOOD

A diet of nectar alone will not be sufficient to keep a hummingbird healthy. It will also need protein for growth and some fat to provide an additional source of energy and an insulating layer beneath the skin. Protein and fat are usually obtained by feeding on insects. Most hummingbirds are seen to chase and catch insects many times during the day. Insects are often found feeding around the plants that

The protruding anthers of the gooseberry flowers dust pollen on the chin of this Anna's hummingbird as it feeds. It will transfer the pollen to the next flower it feeds on, thus carrying out cross pollination.

provide the hummingbird's nectar, so they are easily located and caught, but others are found at some distance, perhaps over a stream or visiting another species of flower unsuitable as a hummingbird's food plant. Here the hummingbird will make rapid flights to and fro with its head turning skilfully in all directions so it can snap up as many insects as possible. Tiny spiders will also be eaten, sometimes being plucked from leaves and sometimes taken as spiderlings from their protective cocoons, and insects caught in spider's webs may be plucked from the web before the spider can get to them. Several hundred insects and other invertebrates will be taken every day. These too are digested very speedily. The time taken for the indigestible remains, such as wing cases and legs, to pass through the digestive tract and appear in the droppings is about 20 minutes.

Many of the straight-billed species of hummingbirds feed by 'hawking', that is, pursuing airborne insects from a perch. Some use a high perch, like flycatchers do, and dart from it to catch an individual insect, while others sit in more concealed positions in the foliage and shoot out to catch insects as they fly past. Both the Green-tailed train-bearer and the Buff-tailed coronet feed on insects by hawking. The hermit hummingbirds catch their insects by 'gleaning': they search the vegetation thoroughly, hovering under the leaves, inspecting every tiny flower and

The tongue of this Allen's hummingbird is protruding slightly as it approaches a flower to feed.

watching for any flicker of movement. They pick individual insects skilfully from the plants.

At least three species of hummingbirds living at very high altitudes in the Andes have been seen feeding on the ground, although it is not always clear if this activity is in search of ground-dwelling insects, such as ants, or to collect nectar from the very low-growing plants typical of high mountain slopes and exposed plateaus. The Olivaceous thornbill has been observed collecting nectar from low-growing flowers at about 14,000 feet (4250 m) in Peru and Bolivia by perching on the plants. The low oxygen levels at high altitudes make an energetic activity like hovering very difficult to sustain for long periods, so the scrambling technique has been adopted as it is much more energy efficient. The Bearded helmetcrest also is seen to feed like this from time to time.

Ground feeding has also been observed in Allen's hummingbird in California. What is not clear about this observation is whether the bird is seeking insects like ants and beetles on the ground or collecting tiny particles of grit for the gizzard. Birds need an abrasive substance in the gizzard to help break down tough materials in the food that they eat, like the chitinous cuticles of insects, and the grit needs to be replaced regularly. Calcium is also required for the production of egg shells, and this is sometimes obtained from grit.

In addition to energy and growth foods, the hummingbird will also need vitamins and minerals in order to maintain its health. These will normally be obtained from its food

The Sword-billed hummingbird, with its long, straight bill, has the longest of all hummingbird bills.

providing its diet has plenty of variety. Birds in captivity, which are usually dependent upon artificial foods, may suffer from a lack of vitamins and minerals. It is therefore important that the correct supplements are added to their food. Water is important too, and this is obtained from the nectar, which in some flowers can be quite dilute, from streams, rivers, pools, dew on leaves, and often from bird feeders.

When feeding on insects the bill is normally used in the same way that we would use a pair of forceps; insects are plucked individually from the air and then swallowed. It would take us a lot longer to catch a meal of insects with forceps, however, than it does the hummingbird, aided as it is by its keen eyesight and expert flight!

Because the flight is so rapid and the insects so small, there were many erroneous ideas in the past about how the hummingbird actually managed to catch its prey. It was thought that the long tongue was flicked out in the same way that a toad feeds and that the insects were trapped by getting stuck to its surface. However, studies on captive birds have since shown that the surface of the tongue is not sticky and that insects will actually fall off it if the tongue is not quickly withdrawn.

It was also suggested that some hummingbirds spat a droplet of sticky saliva at an insect, in a similar fashion to a feeding archer fish, and then caught the insect as it fell out of the sky. It is only through patient and close observations that our present knowledge has been built up and that we now know how the bill is used.

THE BILL AND TONGUE

Hummingbirds lack the gaping mouths of their near relatives, the swifts, and they do not have the same bristle-like structures around the mouth which flycatchers use to prevent insects from escaping. They more than compensate for these deficiencies, however, by their skill in the air, and they are easily able to out-maneuver flying insects and catch them in their slender bills.

The typical hummingbird bill is a slender, pointed structure which can probe the corolla tubes of flowers. However, during the course of evolution this basic structure has been modified to enable the birds to exploit various sources of nectar. Some species have general purpose bills that are of use in a variety of flowers, being able to probe quite long nectar tubes and also the shorter tubes in composite flowers such as daisies.

Others show remarkable adaptations to individual flowers. The most striking and well-known example is the bill of the Andean sword-billed hummingbird, which measures about $3\frac{1}{4}$ inches (83 mm) long. With great skill the Sword-billed hummingbird is able to insert this unwieldy structure into the very long corolla tubes of a species of passion flower, *Passiflora mixta*, and yet it is able to use this bill also to build its nest and feed its young. The corolla tube of *Passiflora mixta* is on average $4\frac{1}{4}$ inches (114 mm) long, and so the Sword-bill must also use its tongue to be able to reach the nectar. It is unlikely that any other hummingbird, and certainly any insect, can reach the nectar at the base of such an

The Rainbow-bearded thornbill has one of the shortest bills of all hummingbirds; it can be used for piercing flowers to obtain the nectar as well as feeding in the normal way.

elongated corolla tube, so only the Sword-bill, with its extra long bill and extensible tongue, can make use of it. This is an excellent example of how bird and flower have evolved together.

The White-tipped sickle-bill and the Hairy hermit both have bills of moderate length which are beautifully curved so that they can fit into the flowers of the various species of *Heliconia* common in tropical regions. The tiny Purple-backed thornbill has the shortest hummingbird bill of all at less than half an inch (1 cm) long, and it is able to make use of the nectar provided by the tiny flowers of various composites, such as daisies. In a few cases the bill is actually upturned at the tip,

such as in the Fiery-tailed awlbill and the Mountain avocetbill. The nostrils at the base of the bill are protected by a scale-like structure which may help to prevent pollen grains from entering the breathing tubes when the bird is feeding.

The bill alone would not be sufficient for collecting nectar from flowers; the hummingbird also has a specially modified tongue to help it feed. This organ is more difficult to study as it does not show at all when the hummingbird is feeding. A perched bird sometimes flicks its tongue out momentarily, and its length can be surprising. It is normally as long as the bill and often white in color. The tongue has two halves to it, and these unite to form a tube along which nectar can be sucked. At the base of the tongue are powerful muscles which are used to push it outwards, and along its length are more muscles and a membrane, the function of which is not fully understood. In some species the tip of the tongue supports many brush-like bristles which absorb nectar and make its collection easier.

FLOWERS AND POLLINATION

Hummingbirds are attracted to a wide range of flowers, but they are particularly interested in those whose petals are predominantly red. Indeed, red is such an attraction to them that

in their never-ending search for nectar they will investigate a variety of other red objects, including patterned clothing, red ear-rings, flowery wallpaper inside rooms, and many unlikely man-made objects like red stop switches on lawn mowers. They take readily to artificial nectar feeders which have a rosette of red plastic resembling a flower placed around the opening.

During the course of evolution both hummingbirds and flowers have developed elaborate mechanisms to ensure that each one

The bill of the Tooth-billed hummingbird is unusual among hummingbirds, and indeed birds in general, being slightly upturned at the tip.

Bromeliads growing in tropical forests are ornithophilous, that is they produce conspicuous red flowers in order to attract hummingbirds rather than insects.

survives. It is vitally important to the flowers that they are visited by hummingbirds, just as it is vital to the birds to obtain nectar from flowers for energy. The nectar is offered in return for the hummingbirds' services as pollinators. When pollen is transferred from flower to flower, fertilization takes place and seeds will be produced, thus ensuring the continuation of that plant species into the next generation. As the hummingbird flits from flower to flower, it will carry pollen grains with it, some stuck to the base of the bill, and some clinging to its feathers.

To ensure that it is hummingbirds which visit and not insects, which would not effect pollination, many flowers have developed long nectar-tubes that can only be probed by the long bill of a bird. Sometimes the nectar can be reached by the tip of the bill when the hummingbird is hovering in front of the flower, but in some species it is necessary for the bird to push its head deep inside the flower in order to reach the nectaries at the base of the petals. After feeding in this way the hummingbird often leaves the flower with its head lightly dusted with golden pollen grains. The next flower it visits may trap these pollen grains, and thus cross-pollination will have been carried out and the hummingbird will have earned its nectar. Flowers in the *Heliconia* and *Passiflora* families show a range

The reflexed petals of the Passion flower make it difficult for insects to land and steal the nectar, but the anthers are in the perfect position to deposit pollen on the head of the Bronzy hermit hummingbird.

The Bronze-tailed plumeleteer makes use of the bracts of Heliconia sarapiquensis, *a typical hummingbird-pollinated flower, as a perch when collecting nectar.*

of adaptations to ensure pollination by hummingbirds, and the bromeliads and members of the *Gesneriaceae* are also commonly pollinated by hummingbirds. The flowers of *Heliconia bihai* have a degree of curvature which exactly matches the curved bills of the Hairy hermit and Green hermit.

The typical hummingbird flower is one that flowers during the day, normally has radial symmetry – that is, the petals are arranged in an open rosette – or possibly has an overhanging 'hood', produces copious nectar, but has no scent. The anthers, or pollen-producing structures, will protrude from the flower in such a way that they will touch the head of a bird collecting nectar, and the stigma will be in a similar position, ready to collect pollen from a feeding bird. The flower will normally be in a prominent position, either held horizontally or hanging downwards, and the petals will be recurved, to prevent insects from landing on them. The corolla tube will be strengthened to prevent the bird's bill from damaging it and possibly to make it more difficult for the flower piercers to penetrate the base of the tube.

Many flowers in the United States are ornithophilous; that is, they are designed to be pollinated by hummingbirds. About 19 species of flowers have been identified as being ornithophilous east of the Rockies, while in the west, where there is a greater range of hummingbird species, there are many more. Further south, in Central America and the tropics, there are a great many more, and they show a wider range of adaptations to the variety of hummingbird bill shapes. Insect-pollinated flowers normally have a strong scent and are often provided with 'landing stages' in the form of horizontally arranged petals. Many of them will have blue or yellow coloration instead of red which is not easily detected by insects. In the eastern hemisphere, where there are no hummingbirds and no bird-pollinated flowers, there is a smaller proportion of red flowers in the native flora, whereas in the western hemisphere, where bird pollination is important, there is a much higher proportion of red coloration in flowers.

Experimental work has indicated that hummingbirds learn to associate the color of a particular flower with the supply of food.

Taste does not seem to be an important factor in choosing any particular species as a food source. Walter Scheithauer offered a captive hummingbird a sugar solution that had been given an unpleasant bitter taste. At first the bird rejected it, but later, when hunger took over, the bird fed in the normal way without any sign of distaste. What seems to be more important is the regularity and abundance of the supply, and the actual concentration of sugar in the nectar. Both glucose and fructose are available in nectar in different species, and there seems to be no preference here either.

In some cases the flower does not achieve pollination in return for its nectar, as some species of hummingbirds have learnt how to bypass the pollen-producing anthers at the mouth of the flower and make straight for the nectaries. To do this, the Purple-crowned fairy pushes its short, but extremely sharp bill straight through the corolla tube at the base of the flower, as if it was using a hypodermic needle, and extracts the nectar direct from the nectaries. The forward thrust generated by its whirring wings is strong enough to enable it to penetrate even quite tough corollas.

In addition to visiting flowers, some species will drink the sugary sap that oozes from cuts in tree bark or from holes made by sap-sucking woodpeckers, and occasionally juicy or squashed fruits are investigated, although this may be in search of insects which are also attracted by the sugar.

The Long-tailed hermit's bill is curved to fit easily into the corolla of its food plants.

Feeding in captivity

Early attempts to keep hummingbirds in captivity always failed because the true nature of their diet was not understood. They were provided with food consisting solely of nectar or sugar solutions. After a few days they would invariably lose their vigor and then slowly deteriorate and die. Given weak sugar solutions, they would feed for a very long time each day in order to obtain sufficient energy, whereas strong sugar solutions caused them to seek water as well. The addition of a few vitamins to the sugar diet helped a little, but it was not until captive hummingbirds were offered protein foods that they could be kept for any length of time. This food was often in the form of a solution or fine suspension of eggs, fish meal or other animal products. However, the common fruit fly, *Drosophila melanogaster*, so easily cultured and frequently used in genetics investigations, proved to be an acceptable substitute for a normal diet. The major breakthrough in feeding hummingbirds an artificial diet and keeping them for lengthy periods in captivity allowed many observers to study them at close quarters and added greatly to our understanding of these fascinating birds.

Some early ornithologists assumed that insects alone were the reason hummingbirds visited flowers. Large numbers of the birds were shot as they fed around flowers, and after dissection, their stomach contents were examined under a microscope. Inside were found the remains of many insects and spiders, thus convincing the ornithologists

that these were their main, if not their only food. They failed to realize that the nectar would have passed rapidly into the hummingbird's intestines and then be absorbed into the blood stream without leaving any traces in the stomach at all.

Walter Scheithauer's painstaking studies on captive hummingbirds in Europe in the 1960s yielded a great deal of valuable information which has enabled many aviculturists to keep them in good health and even encourage them to nest successfully. He tried feeding a bird on honey solution alone, allowing it no access to insect food. After only one day on this diet a male White-eared hummingbird became listless and unwell. When the diet was supplemented with a limitless supply of insects in the form of fruit flies, there was a rapid recovery to full health and vitality. The bird still consumed mostly energy-rich carbohydrates, but it obviously benefited from the addition of insect food. When the honey solution was enriched with egg-yolk, milk powder, blood serum, bananas, and mealworms, the White-ear looked decidedly unwell. Obviously suffering from an excess of fat and protein the bird spent more time perching at the end of the day than was normal. Just as we may sometimes need to sleep off a heavy meal of roast pork, the hummingbird too had to allow plenty of time for its unusually heavy meal of fats and proteins to be digested. After further investigations, Walter Scheithauer concluded that a food solution comprising four times the bird's body weight in water, 70 per cent of its weight in honey, 3 per cent protein, 2 per cent fat, and 6 per cent vitamins, minerals, and fibre was the most satisfactory.

WATCHING HUMMINGBIRDS IN THE GARDEN

Hummingbirds can be studied at close quarters without the need to keep them in captivity. Over much of the United States they are frequent visitors to yards and gardens. A hummingbird may pay a brief visit to investigate possible sources of food, find things not to its liking and disappear for good. Sometimes it may stay around and even settle down to breed.

There is plenty that can be done by the enthusiastic gardener to encourage the hummingbird to stay; the most important is to provide some food. This can be in the form of an artificial diet offered in a nectar feeder. The feeder will need a colorful rosette placed around its mouth to attract the attention of a hummingbird at first, but soon there will be no need for this as the bird quickly learns where its food is provided. If the feeder is kept filled there will be some activity around it for most of the day. It should be positioned where the birds can reach it easily, but if it can also be in view of a window it will be possible to observe the birds at close quarters without disturbing them too much.

Remember that the first feeding of the day is vital to the hummingbird after a long night spent roosting without food, so always make sure that the feeder is kept filled and ready for use at dawn. Also, feeding at dusk is essential so that the birds can have sufficient food reserves to last through the night. Artificial feeding is useful where many hummingbirds are competing for a limited supply of natural food. It is important to remember that the birds will come to depend on it, so the supply must not be suddenly stopped, leaving them without a major part of their diet. A nesting bird may be depending on the extra supply of nectar in order to rear her nestlings, and if this is suddenly cut off she may fail to raise them. If you are going on a vacation it is far better to ask a neighbor to continue feeding the birds every day than suddenly to stop altogether. When migration time approaches it is important to gradually reduce the amount of food offered so that the birds are not tempted to stay too long. If they fail to set off on their long journey south early enough, they will be unable to reach their overwintering sites safely. This is especially important for species like the Ruby-throated and Rufous hummingbirds, which may be breeding up to 2000 miles (3200 km) north of their wintering quarters.

In addition to providing artificial feeders the gardener can also provide a variety of natural foods for hummingbirds. Flowers that produce plenty of nectar will attract them, and these same flowers will also make the garden very colorful to look at. Red flowers seem to attract hummingbirds most easily, although many other colors are visited. Often, these showy red flowers have very little scent, as they do not want to attract insects which would steal the nectar but not pollinate them in return. Insects are another important part of a hummingbird's diet, however, so planting flowers that attract small insects will provide them with an additional source of food.

The environmentally aware gardener will not use poisonous sprays indiscriminately; remember that insects are food for hummingbirds so why not leave them to catch your insect pests for you? As it searches for nectar the hummingbird will pick insects from the surface of leaves, pluck them out of the air, seek them out in dense foliage, and even search in greenhouses. It is far better to risk having a few insect pests around than to spray poison and possibly contaminate the birds you wish to attract.

From time to time hummingbirds benefit from man's activities, even though this was not originally the intention. In Costa Rica thick hedgerows have been planted to prevent the cattle from straying. The plant chosen to achieve this is a type of vervain, *Stachytarpheta*. It is a large, straggling shrub which grows speedily to form a dense hedge 10–12 feet ($3\frac{1}{2}$ m) high and which, when mature, is quite impenetrable to cattle. The plant flowers profusely throughout the year, with only a brief flowerless period during the dry season. It is extensively used by the Violet-headed hummingbird, which has directly benefited in this case from man's manipulation of the environment. On a much smaller scale gardeners can achieve this type of improvement to the hummingbird's food supply by thoughtful planting.

Hummingbirds will nest in yards and gardens if there are suitable sites for them.

Slender branches near a source of food are often chosen, so think carefully about where trees and shrubs can be positioned to encourage the birds to use them. If a hummingbird does set up home in a shrub or tree in your garden, take care you don't attract attention to the nest by visiting it too much yourself. There may be predators around who will spot the signs you make as you visit the nest and then raid it when you have gone.

If you are lucky enough to have a hummingbird nesting in your garden, then why not make some notes about its behavior? Most of what we know about the birds has been gleaned from observers who have spent many long hours watching them going about their business in the wild. A notepad and pencil kept by the window will enable you to get your observations down on paper quickly while the facts are still fresh in your mind. How often does a female return to the nest? How long does she spend building, incubating, or feeding her young? How successful is the female at raising her brood, and does she start a second nest in the same season? Which flowers are visited most often, and which seem to provide the best food? What is the male doing while all this is going on? Many useful facts can be gained in this way, and as we increase our knowledge about these birds we will be better equipped to ensure that future generations, too, are able to enjoy them.

A red Gladiolus has attracted an Anna's hummingbird to feed in a garden.

CHAPTER 5

THE HUMMINGBIRD'S DAILY ROUTINE

Bathing · Preening

Aggression and defence

Predators and other dangers

The daily cycle of activities

Sleep

The Spot-throated hummingbird, like many other species, often chooses perches which are over streams.

BATHING

Feeding occupies a large part of a hummingbird's time during daylight hours and this has been dealt with elsewhere. During the breeding season males are pre-occupied with their displays, and females will be busy nest-building, incubating their small clutch of eggs, or raising their young. One other activity occupies hummingbirds for lengthy periods during the day, however, and that is bathing. They seem to take great delight in immersing themselves in shallow pools or flitting through the spray of waterfalls. Garden sprinklers are a great attraction to species such as Anna's hummingbird, while birds in captivity will readily take to small, shallow dishes of water.

In the wild there are many sources of water that can be used for bathing. The Rufous-tailed hummingbird of Ecuador and Venezuela can utilize the film of water collected on broad leaves during a tropical storm. By pressing itself down on the leaf and spreading its wings and tail, it can wet its plumage quite effectively before flying off to a perch to continue preening. The Fork-tailed wood-nymph, widespread over Central and South America, dips its body into pools and streams, using its wings to splash water over its feathers. The Magnificent or Rivoli's hummingbird delights in bathing in the fast-flowing streams of the mountains and canyons of Mexico and the south-western United States, where it breeds. Damp moss on branches in tropical forests provides sufficient moisture for the Scaly-breasted hummingbird, which presses its body down until enough water has been absorbed by the plumage.

Beside a favorite bathing pool or cascading stream there may be hummingbirds to watch nearly all day. What is not clear is how many times during the day one individual may visit the site to bathe. The dashing flights to and from the bathing pools make it very difficult to follow the movements of an individual bird. Observations of birds in captivity have shown that some individuals do make repeated visits to water to bathe, but their behavior in captivity may not reflect their true natural behavior.

PREENING

Preening is very important to birds as it maintains their plumage in efficient working order. Feathers must provide insulation, camouflage or display markings, and the means of flight, so they must be kept in good condition at all times. The bill is the main structure used in preening, and it is run through the feathers repeatedly, arranging the interlocking barbules and keeping all the feathers in their normal overlapping positions. At the base of the tail is a preen gland which produces an oily substance. When rubbed over the feathers, this provides waterproofing, so all birds frequently rub their bills or the backs of their heads onto the

This Paraguayan greenback indulges in wing-stretching whilst perched.

preen gland and then distribute the oil picked up on them over the rest of their plumage.

Birds with very long bills find great difficulty in reaching all their feathers, so they have to resort to scratching with their feet. The back of the head and the throat are out of reach whatever the length of bill, so all hummingbirds have to lower a wing and raise a foot over it to reach the head or throat. This indirect scratching is common to all hummingbirds, but some species of passerines, such as the finches, are able to reach their heads with their feet without having to lower their wings – a method known as direct scratching. Some long-billed birds, such as ibises, solve the problem of preening the head and neck by engaging in mutual preening. These highly social, colonial species carry out many activities in groups, but not so the hummingbirds. A little mutual preening and scratching has been observed in nestling hummingbirds, but not once they have fledged.

AGGRESSION AND DEFENCE

Hummingbirds have an undeserved reputation for aggressiveness towards each other. Although they are in no way social species they do engage in some communal activities, such as the singing assemblies of the male hermits or the communal roosting of the Chimborazo hillstars. They are often seen chasing each other, but these pursuits may be nothing more than a form of play. Rival males at assembly areas sometimes make short dashes to warn intruders away from a favorite perch, but these assemblies would not work at all if they were totally antagonistic towards each other. In captivity hummingbirds seem to do best in mixed groups in large aviaries. Although even here they do not engage in mutual preening or roost close together for warmth, they do indulge in frequent skirmishes and chases and seem to thrive on the presence of other birds. Solitary hummingbirds rarely seem as lively as those provided with companions. The birds will roost in mixed groups, but they do not sit close enough together to touch each other or provide body heat, even on a cold night.

Intruders that pose a real threat to the safety of nestlings or to a good source of food are treated rather differently, however. The needle-like bill of the Ruby-throated hummingbird is quite a threatening weapon when thrust forward by a powerful little body on whirring wings. The hummingbird can adopt an aggressive posture that is recognized as a threat by most other birds. Even farmyard chickens have been driven away by an attacking Ruby-throat! Walter Scheithauer presented an incubating Brown inca in his aviary with a stuffed Long-eared owl, and there was an immediate reaction. The plumage was fluffed up to make the bird look

Brown Incas have not been observed very well in their wild habitat in the northern Andes, but they have been studied in avaries where they prove to be active and aggressive. They use the long bill as a threat to warn other hummingbirds away from a good food source.

larger, and the head and bill were thrust forward towards the giant predator. This aggressive posture was accompanied by shrill twitterings which were obviously intended to intimidate the potential enemy. In common with many small birds, hummingbirds will mob predators by flying around them calling noisily. Often, if a commotion is heard in a forest it will be caused by a mixed flock of small birds which have discovered a sitting owl or large hawk and are all calling excitedly around it. In these mixed gatherings it is often the hummingbirds that will venture closest and remain for the longest time to taunt the enemy. Repeated false stabs with the tiny bill will often drive a much larger bird to seek cover away from its tiny adversaries.

PREDATORS AND OTHER DANGERS

It is unusual for a hummingbird to be taken by a bird of prey, but there are some records of them having been taken by some of the smaller raptors, such as the American kestrel and Sharp-shinned hawk. These raptors are able to approach quickly and quietly and surprise an unsuspecting hummingbird while it is feeding. Raptors used to hunting in woodland are more able to take an alert, agile bird like a hummingbird than are some of the

Perching on thistles can sometimes be dangerous because of the risk of being trapped by the spines, but this male Rufous hummingbird is sitting safely on the flower head.

larger birds of prey more suited to hunting in the open.

There are other predators, however, which have also been seen to take hummingbirds. Feeding near a pond or bathing brings hummingbirds within range of large frogs which, being perfectly capable of capturing large insects like water beetles or dragonflies, find it quite easy to catch a small bird. Fish such as the bass are also able to catch small birds if they hover too close to the water. Dragonflies have been seen pursuing Ruby-throated hummingbirds, although this may be more to do with seeing off a potential rival for food. The Praying mantis normally lies motionless and camouflaged in wait for its insect prey in bushes and shrubs. If a hummingbird comes too close it may be at risk. Again, the Ruby-throat seems to have been a victim of mantids at times.

Although they have excellent eyesight and very good reflexes, hummingbirds in flight do occasionally blunder into things that can cause them some harm. Tough spider's webs can entangle small species, and there are records of hummingbirds having been caught in cobwebs and becoming so badly trapped that the spider has been able to wrap the helpless bird in silk and suck its blood for a meal later on. Some plants have spines and prickles that can injure or even trap hummingbirds. There are instances of Ruby-throats having been caught in thistle heads and remaining stuck until they died. Burdock and some tough grasses also have hooks or bristles which can trap birds so securely that they may die.

Plate-glass windows with other windows or mirrors on the opposite wall can cause serious injuries to many birds, including hummingbirds, as they fail to notice the glass and, thinking they can fly straight through to the greenery they can see on the other side, dash themselves into the glass, often with considerable force. Many birds are killed like this, but sometimes they are only stunned and will recover if left in a quiet, warm place for a while. Fine-mesh screens are also a problem if daylight can be seen through them, because hummingbirds will fly at them with their usual speed and drive their needle-sharp bills into the mesh. This is usually done with such force that the birds are unable to extricate themselves and remain there until released, or, sadly, until they die. They need not be trapped for very long to run into difficulties; their energy requirements are so high that if they are deprived of food for even a few minutes they will run out of energy, or they may dehydrate rapidly in the heat of the sun.

Man is usually not treated as a predator or potential threat; in fact some hummingbirds show great curiosity about humans, hovering inquisitively in front of people, giving the impression that they are curious about every aspect of the human countenance. Many birdwatchers claim they have formed close associations with individual hummingbirds. Gardeners often say that a particular bird will

A characteristic roosting posture of the Magnificent hummingbird is to sit with its head and neck erect, giving it a very sleek appearance.

fly up to greet them when they enter the garden or go to the nectar feeder to replenish it. There are claims that migratory species like the Ruby-throat can recognize individual humans year after year as they return to a familiar breeding ground in someone's garden or orchard.

THE DAILY CYCLE OF ACTIVITIES

For a while around midday hummingbirds spend a period of time roosting quietly. Apart from during the night this is one of the few times of day when they are not engaging in some frenzied activity on the wing. In the first few hours of daylight hummingbirds are very active working to restore the food reserves used up during the night. The first priority is to take in some energy-rich foods, so frequent visits will be made to flowers in search of nectar. Breakfast will consist of many small snacks with repeated visits being made to good sources of nectar. There will be lots of frantic chases in mid-air and also several bouts of preening and bathing. Things quiet down around the middle of the day, but as the afternoon passes the activity becomes more frenzied again, and by the time other species of birds have started to go to roost the hummingbirds will be engaged in another bout of feeding. They must take in lots of nectar and also seek out insects so that small amounts of fat can also be stored.

Outside the breeding season the day is spent feeding, bathing, preening, engaging in frantic chases, and sitting quietly, although,

whatever hummingbirds do, they seem to do it with far more energy and style than any other bird.

SLEEP

When the hummingbirds finally settle on their roosting perches they prepare for the night by lowering their body temperature to within a few degrees of the air temperature. Some species actually ruffle their feathers to expose their skin to the air to speed the dissipation of heat. As the bird descends into torpor it will settle on its perch into a characteristic sleep posture. The head tilts backwards, and the bill is pointed towards the sky. Once in the torpid state the hummingbird will not respond to any stimuli like sudden noises or movements near its perch. It is only the rise in temperature and increase in light at dawn that will raise it from the torpid state back to its normal rate of activity, when it will commence feeding again. The word noctivation has been used to describe this overnight torpidity, and it is similar to the much longer period of inactivity carried out by many mammals in winter known as hibernation, when all bodily functions slow down in order to save energy.

In common with many other species, the Long-tailed sylph roosts with its head tilted backwards and its bill pointing towards the sky.

This male Allen's hummingbird is ruffling his feathers prior to roosting for the night.

CHAPTER 6

BREEDING

Courtship · Nest building

Egg laying and incubation

Nest predation

Care of the nestlings

Two nestling Broad-tailed hummingbirds begin to outgrow their nest.

COURTSHIP

The sole function of the male in the breeding process in hummingbirds is to fertilize the female. With one or two exceptions he plays no part in nest-building, incubating the eggs, feeding the young or protecting his offspring. His energies are devoted entirely to attracting and courting the female. To this end males of most species of hummingbirds have evolved some elaborate courtship displays and brilliant adornments to their plumage.

There are two main methods used by male hummingbirds to attract females. Dazzling plumage coupled with eye-catching display flights can be used effectively by those species which live in fairly open habitats, while song is used by the species living in dense vegetation such as the understorey of tropical forests. As a general rule the forest-dwelling species which use song to attract their mates have subdued coloration and few adornments like crests or tail streamers, whereas open-country species have many elaborate display features such as iridescent throat-patches, greatly extended tails, and exciting flight patterns. The open-country species may also use sounds in their courtship; the voice may be used, but certainly the humming sounds of the wings often increase dramatically as frenzied swoops and dives take place.

A hummingbird's voice is rather weak, so if song is important in its courtship it is to its advantage to combine its efforts with those of other individuals of the same species. Many tropical species form assemblies where their combined vocalisations act as a greater attraction to females than might the feeble song of an individual. These assemblies often take place at sites that are used year after year, and females come to associate them with finding a choice of males. Various species of violet-ears, such as the White-vented and Brown, have quite loud songs, and when they are singing in large assemblies theirs may be the dominant sounds heard in the forest. Large assembly areas may stretch for 220 yards (200 m) or more through suitable parts of the forest. Often it is only a drastic change in the habitat, such as a fire or the falling of a tree, which will lead to the abandoning of a traditional site in favor of a new one. One Long-tailed hermit assembly area in a forest in Guyana was observed for 12 years in succession before the birds finally deserted it. It may well have been functioning for several years before that. Although up to 100 singing males may be found in one assembly area, there may be large tracts of forest where none are found at all. These may well be the quiet areas that females will choose as nesting sites, free from disturbance and the conspicuous attention-drawing males.

Communal displays by males are the normal method of courtship in the hermits, hummingbirds typical of dense tropical woodland. Each male perches on a favorite twig, perhaps only a few feet above the ground, and when still he is very difficult to see as his drab, brown coloration blends well

The Terra Firme rainforest of the Amazon basin provides an ideal nesting habitat for hermit hummingbirds.

with a background of leaf debris. His wagging tail, however, showing flashes of white, does attract attention. Both the Blue-throated golden-tail and the Violet-headed hummingbird are more brightly marked than the hermits, and they perform higher up in the canopy, while the White-eared hummingbird flits from high to low perches throughout his display.

Each male seems to prefer his own perch, no matter how many other males there are nearby. Just occasionally one male invades the territory of another, provoking a flurry of activity. The interloper will be driven away, and after a short aerial skirmish both birds will return to their rightful perches and resume their songs.

Singing occurs throughout the year, but for each individual species it precedes its nesting season and ceases once all the females have mated and are busy rearing their young, so although there may always be male hummingbirds displaying in a particular forest, it will only be those species that are actually breeding which will be active.

The Rufous-tailed hummingbird starts to sing in the grey light of dawn before the sun has risen, and once the sunlight has penetrated the foliage it becomes silent for the rest of the day, but some species, including the hermits, sing throughout the day with little diminution of their energy. They may make brief pauses to visit nearby flowers for a little nectar, but they soon return to their song-perches to continue in their efforts to impress a prospective mate. Others, like the Blue-chested hummingbird, have two distinct song

periods during the day with separate bouts of singing in the morning and evening, sometimes increasing the length of the song periods so much that they too are active for almost the whole day. Although the male hummingbird does not assist the female at all, he probably spends as much time displaying during the breeding season as she does in nest-building and rearing her young.

The Calliope hummingbird's name means the 'sweet-voiced' little star. This is rather puzzling as its voice is not particularly sweet, nor is it very audible. During his elaborate display flight in which the male makes U-shaped swoops over distances of about 30 feet (9 m), he will utter the occasional 'bzzt' sound, and other faint twitterings are made while feeding, but no real song is ever produced.

A female who responds to a particular male may stimulate an even more frantic display which to human eyes is very difficult to interpret. A frenzied flight through the surrounding vegetation is presumably followed by mating, although this act has rarely been witnessed in the wild. In the case of the Andean hillstar the female has been seen to offer food to the male as a response to his display. This is probably an indication to the male that the female is receptive and mating will follow.

A number of other species of birds, totally unrelated to the hummingbirds, engage in communal displays by the males. Many of the gamebirds, such as grouse, form leks in which males strut and crow in order to impress the watching females. Prominent features like bright under-tail feathers are displayed at these leks and the females make their choice of male before mating. Unlike the hummingbirds, gamebirds normally mate at or very near to the lek.

There are some observations of mating between the males and females of different species. Where this has been followed by egg-laying the result has often been infertile eggs. If offspring do result from a mixed mating they are almost always infertile, so the hybrid is not perpetuated.

NEST BUILDING

The female hummingbird is at her most vulnerable when sitting on her nest incubating the small clutch of eggs or brooding her nestlings. For this reason the nests of most species are very well concealed and extremely difficult to find. Overhanging leaves are a common hiding place but many other sites are utilized, ranging from forks in tiny branches to caves and rock overhangs.

One thing is common to all hummingbird nests; they are all incredibly small! The nest of the Bee hummingbird from Cuba is smaller than a half walnut shell, and in many species the nests are rarely more than an inch ($2\frac{1}{2}$ cm) across. This small size coupled with the secretive location contributes to the security of the nest and the incubating female.

Finding a suitable nesting site and building the nest are both the responsibility of the female. She will investigate many possible sites within her home range, settling on tiny

All hummingbird nests are very small; this Calliope hummingbird's nest clearly illustrates this.

branches, flitting below leaves and investigating likely perches from every possible angle. After one or two false starts she will finally settle on one site. Nests are never built on the ground, but they may be as low as one or two feet (30–50 cm) above ground level if there is no taller vegetation available.

The Sapphire-throated hummingbird usually chooses a low nest site such as the fork below the dead flower of an herbaceous plant which projects a short distance above the grasses around it. The nest will be built from downy plant fibres, dead leaves and seeds, and a few lichens, and when completed will be very difficult to see. Nests have been found as high as 30 feet (9 m) above the ground in

tropical forests where there is a dense canopy. The nest site will normally be located well away from other hummingbirds; it is unusual to find two nests close together. Also, the nest will be out of sight of displaying males whose amorous activities may attract the attention of predators.

In the case of the Chimborazo hillstars living high up on the slopes of the Cotopaxi volcano in Ecuador, the sometimes appalling weather conditions below the ice-capped summit drive them to seek protection in caves and rock crevices. If there is severely limited availability of suitable sites, several nests may be found close together. Surviving the freezing night-time temperatures or avoiding driving snow is more important than keeping a great distance between nests. This is an interesting parallel with the swifts, which often nest in colonies in caves.

The Rufous hummingbird occasionally nests in something approaching a small colony, when about ten nests may be found in a small area, some of them only a few yards from their nearest neighbor.

Having chosen the correct spot the female then begins the quest for nesting material. For nests suspended below leaves a few long threads are required to act as a sling to support the remainder of the nest. A variety of materials can be used for this initial stage in the construction. Fine grasses and animal and

The female Hairy hermit uses cobwebs, grasses, lichens and leaves to construct her nest. It is suspended below a leaf for added protection.

even human hair can be utilized, although cobwebs are most commonly used.

The nest-building female gives a spectacular display of aerobatics as she builds her nest, as practically the whole operation is carried out while she is on the wing. All the skills of hummingbird flight are brought into play as the female weaves these long threads over, under, and around the supporting leaf or branch. Her own saliva or some sticky nectar may be used to glue the first few supporting threads to the leaf, and others will then be woven between the anchor threads. Her bill may be used like a sewing needle, pushing threads through the growing nest and then pulling them out on the other side. She flits excitedly from the rapidly growing nest to the surrounding vegetation, investigating every possible source of nesting material.

Captive birds often investigate the heads of their keepers in the hope of finding a few stray threads! Birds nesting in gardens can be encouraged by offering them bundles of suitable materials such as sweepings from the carpet or hairs from the dog's comb. Different species have their favorite types of nesting material, and they will search over a wide area to find enough of it. They will not hesitate to steal from another bird's nest if they happen to find it unoccupied.

Once the initial support has been built, the nest cup itself can be started. This has to be sufficiently deep to support the eggs and the incubating female, and later the growing chicks who will not leave it until they are fully fledged. Soft materials are used in this stage of the process, and the female will search for cobwebs, lichens, feathers, downy seeds and very fine grasses. Lichens are frequently used on the outside of the nest, no doubt serving to camouflage it, and they are also used to make a soft lining for the base of the cup in some nests. Tufts of moss, the fine fibers from the unrolling fronds of ferns, wisps of animal fur caught in thorns and even stray man-made fibers have all been found in hummingbirds' nests.

The Long-tailed hermit suspends her nest below the overhanging tip of a palm frond so that the nest cup has a green roof above it. Starting the construction of the nest here is very difficult as there is nothing for the female to perch on. She must work on the wing at first, flying round and round the tip of the leaf carefully weaving cobwebs into a loop. They may be secured by saliva or nectar, and then she will start to add lichens, mosses, or downy seeds to form a shallow saucer; using the weight of her body she sits in the saucer and depresses it into a tiny cup. As the nest cup grows, wisps of the nesting material hang below it like long streamers, sometimes offering the only clue to the nest's where-abouts beneath the leaf. In natural forest habitats there is a plentiful supply of large leaves of this type, but when the forest is cleared and replanted with agricultural crops the palms and wild bananas that produce the broad leaves will be absent. Although the plants under cultivation may provide nectar, and possibly even attract insects, the absence of suitable nesting sites causes the hermits to abandon the area altogether.

In Venezuela, the Sooty-capped hermit builds an extraordinary nest which is suspended by a single woven strand of cobweb from an overhead branch or leaf. The supporting strand is attached to the rim of the nest cup at a single point, which makes it unbalanced, especially when the bird is sitting. To compensate for this the nest is counter-balanced by tiny weights, usually in the form of pellets of dried clay or pieces of grit which are secured to the underside of the nest, just below the point where the supporting cable is attached. Normally found hanging beneath branches, the Sooty-capped hermit's nests have also been seen below bridges and even inside buildings.

As the female hummingbird brings more and more materials to the nest, she weaves them skilfully together and molds the nest cup to fit the shape of her body. She twists and turns in the nest cup, and probably treads the inner lining down with her feet, although this is impossible to see. The shuffling movements she makes suggest that this is what is happening inside the nest. The rim of the nest is finally turned in slightly so that when the female is sitting on her eggs the nesting materials just overlap her wings. This will also prevent the eggs or tiny nestlings from being thrown out of the nest if they are on a branch being swayed by the wind when the female is absent. The whole nest-building process takes several days, and in some cases it may be as

The female Costa's hummingbird is very well camouflaged when she is incubating.

long as a week, during which time the male will be nowhere to be seen.

In some tropical regions where the air is warm but humid, insulation is not such a major consideration, and species such as the Band-tailed barbthroat select nesting materials which give a much more open construction to the nest. Thin rootlets and sparse mosses are chosen, and it is usually possible to see daylight through gaps in the nest walls. If there is a sudden downpour the nest material is less likely to soak up excess moisture and cause problems by chilling the eggs or nestlings. Water can drain away quickly, and the warm air will prevent the nestlings from suffering a drop in body temperature.

The Blue-throated, or Long-tailed sylph, builds a nest with a woven grass roof and a long tail of grasses spilling from the rim. Mosses and lichens are incorporated into the sides, making it a very secure and snug home for the nestlings. A tiny platform of grasses at the rim provides a landing stage for the female when she returns to feed her young.

There are examples of new nests being constructed on top of old nests. This has been recorded several times in studies of the Rufous hummingbird nesting in pine forests in the north-western United States. Up to three nests have been found piled on top of each other. If the original nest is destroyed by a storm or a predator, the Rufous will construct a new one fairly quickly, but this time it will be more skilfully concealed; it may be built in dense foliage or higher up the tree. There is also some seasonal variation in the choice of nest site in the Rufous, with early season nests being constructed in conifers at fairly low levels, and late season nests being built higher up in the canopies of deciduous trees. It is thought that the higher temperatures of late summer may lead to overheating of the nestlings, so the cooling effect of transpiration from deciduous leaves may be beneficial here.

Whatever species is involved, the completed nest of a hummingbird is one of the most fascinating structures in the animal kingdom. Its small size, beautiful construction, and great efficiency in protecting eggs and nestlings is a tribute to the skills of such a tiny builder.

EGG LAYING AND INCUBATION

Having completed her nest the female must now lay her eggs. The normal clutch size for nearly all hummingbirds is two eggs. If more than two are found in a nest, they will be the result of egg laying by more than one female. This is commonest in some of the hermits, whose rather more conspicuous nests, suspended below leaves, often attract the attention of other hummingbirds. The Giant hummingbird lays only a single egg in a nest which, though typical in appearance of other hummingbirds' nests, seems to be a size too small for comfort. Hummingbirds' eggs are the smallest birds' eggs in the world. The Bee hummingbird's eggs are only one third of an inch long, weighing about a quarter of a gram (1/100th oz) each. Although the eggs are minute by comparison with most other birds' eggs, they are very large in proportion to the size of the hummingbird's body. They represent about 10 per cent of the bird's body weight. By comparison, the vast eggs of an Ostrich represent a much smaller proportion of the bird's body weight, and the production of its clutch of 12–15 eggs does not require the same expenditure of energy relative to body size as does that of the hummingbird's two eggs. All hummingbirds' eggs are pure white and often have a shiny, porcelain-like surface.

Incubating the eggs is the responsibility of the female alone, and she will sit for an average of 18 days until they hatch. The White-eared hummingbird has an incubation period of as little as 14 days, but the Andean hillstar has to sit for as long as 23 days. An interesting comparison is with the farmyard hen's egg, which, although it is many times larger than a hummingbird's egg, takes only 21 days to hatch. During incubation the female hummingbird will sit for periods of up to three hours, leaving for short bursts of feeding and bathing. Some species seem reluctant to leave the nest at all during the day, going away from it only for very short periods, perhaps of only a few minutes at a time, whereas others may leave the eggs for as long as half an hour. The female will not wander far from the nest, and any signs of intrusion or disturbance will bring her back at once to defend her brood. Exceptionally, male Sparkling violet-ears have been found incubating, and unlike other hummingbirds the sexes are very similar.

The Long-tailed hermit looks most un-comfortable when she is incubating as the

When incubating, the female Hairy hermit is forced to sit with her head stretched backwards.

Incubation often starts after the laying of the first egg, so hatching can be staggered. One Calliope chick has emerged here, about a day before the other egg is due to hatch.

In some species incubation starts immediately after the first egg has been laid. If there is the usual interval of two days between the laying of the first and second eggs, there will be a corresponding difference in the time of hatching. This means that as the nestlings develop there will always be a size difference between them.

The first egg may even be laid before the construction of the nest is completed; the female may continue to bring materials to the nest and raise its rim as she begins the process of incubation.

The Rufous-breasted hermit has a protracted breeding season, with nests containing eggs having been found almost throughout the year. In Surinam, where this species is common, food is freely available over a long period, so it will easily be possible to raise at least two broods in one year.

From time to time it is necessary to turn the eggs to prevent the embryos becoming attached to the membrane inside the shell. This is achieved on the wing; the sitting bird vibrates her wings rapidly, rises up slightly from the eggs, rotates her body and at the same time moves the eggs with her feet, and then settles again in her original position but with the eggs in their new positions beneath her.

Another activity that takes place during the incubation period is the replenishment of the nesting material. Cobwebs are frequently brought back to the nest, and these help to secure it to its perch. This is especially important to species that nest under slippery structures such as overhanging leaves. Lichens

normal nest site below an overhanging leaf leaves very little room for her to stretch out. She flies in and lands on the eggs with her head towards the overhanging leaf, and to accommodate her long, curved bill the head must be bent backwards. She maintains this seemingly awkward position for two to three hours at a time and can fly off immediately without any apparent signs of discomfort. When leaving the nest she has to fly off backwards for a few inches before turning on the spot and flying away.

are also added to the nest during the incubation period, with this activity taking place mostly during the early morning.

The incubating and brooding females do not become torpid at night. It is important for the eggs to be kept at a constant temperature if the embryos are to develop properly. Nestling hummingbirds do not become torpid either; it is easier for them to maintain a high body temperature because they receive good insulation from the nest and body heat from their mother, who will spend much of the time brooding them.

An interesting example of the way in which changes in temperature can affect hatching was found in the Mato Grosso of Brazil. A nest of the Fork-tailed woodnymph was abandoned by the female after an exceptionally heavy downpour, but as the nest was located in a study area it was observed for some time afterwards, and, surprisingly, 50 hours after the female had deserted her nest the eggs hatched, even though they had not been incubated at all during that time. Presumably the ability of hummingbirds to cope with heterothermy, or different body temperatures, enabled the embryos to continue their development without the need for additional heat. A certain amount of metabolic heat would be produced by the tiny embryos inside the eggs as they respired, and the nest cup would provide some useful insulation. The warm tropical nights would also help to prevent the eggs from becoming severely chilled. The Fork-tailed is the commonest of 13 species of woodnymph found in dark, dense rain forests. They are all difficult to see, and normally it is only through trapping them in fine mist nets as they forage through the undergrowth that any idea can be obtained about their abundance.

NEST PREDATION

Nests do get raided from time to time by a variety of predators. Some species of snakes are able to reach nests on the flimsiest of branches, and no amount of agitated shrieking and diving by the female will deter an intruding snake. Birds like toucans, crows and jays are sometimes a problem, but the swaying branches and mobbing of the defending female are often enough to drive them away. Some small mammals, such as weasels, are also thought to be serious predators in certain areas, and bats have been seen taking young hermits from nests suspended below leaves. Many species of ants will attack and devour young hummingbirds in the nest, and there is little their mother can do to protect them. Alexander Skutch reported that out of nine White-eared hummingbird nests which he found in the oak and pine woods of Guatemala at about 8500 feet (2500 m) above sea level, only half of the two eggs per nest actually hatched. Out of the nine nestlings that emerged, only three survived to the fledging stage and flew off from the nest, after which their fortunes were unknown. Some researchers have suggested that predators find nests by watching humans visiting them for photography or to band the

nestlings. Predation can be a problem for birds breeding in temperate regions, where they have a limited amount of time before the end of the summer, but in tropical and equatorial regions a lost clutch of eggs can be replaced without the danger of hard weather setting in before the young are raised.

Care of the nestlings

If all goes well the eggs will hatch, and the female will remove the pieces of eggshell in her beak, fly off for a short distance, and dispose of them. Apart from helping to maintain nest hygiene, this also makes the nest less conspicuous to predators. The newly hatched young look like helpless little grubs. They are blind and featherless, and totally dependent on their mother for food and warmth. This is the time when the well-constructed nest repays all the earlier efforts of the mother. She must leave her nestlings periodically to obtain food, so they need all the insulation they can get from the downy nest and its overhanging rim. The female may cover her nestlings with tiny pieces of lichen or moss as she leaves the nest. Nestling hummingbirds do not develop down as many small birds do at this early stage. Their normal plumage develops slowly, and by the time they are ready to leave the nest they have what looks like an adult plumage.

A female Glittering-bellied emerald perches on the edge of her nest as she feeds nectar to one of her nestlings.

The Long-tailed hermit feeds her young on the wing, without needing to perch on the rim of the nest.

The young hummingbirds are fed on regurgitated food directly from their mother's bill. All her skills of maneuverability, normally used to probe into flowers in search of nectar, are now required to direct the bill into the mouths of her hungry offspring. This is quite an achievement, especially in the case of the Sword-billed hummingbird, whose enormously long bill could damage the delicate throats of her tiny nestlings if used clumsily.

The nectar she feeds them is easily digested and is used by the nestlings to provide the energy to keep warm. They also require protein for growth, and this is supplied in the form of partly digested insects. The female will feed her chicks alternately if two are present in the nest, and she will make several offerings before leaving to collect more food. When the young have been fed, their tiny crops bulge outwards until the food can pass down into the digestive tract.

The female spends some time brooding her nestlings, especially at night, but they are frequently left alone during the day when she is away from the nest searching for food. Even at this time of potential danger the male plays no part in the upbringing of his offsprings.

Nest hygiene is maintained easily as the nestlings will raise themselves up to defecate over the rim and not soil the nest cup. Some rather unpleasant parasites may afflict them, however. Fleas and feather lice are a perennial problem for nesting birds, but the parasitic larvae of small flies may burrow below the nestling's skin, causing unpleasant sores and tumours.

As the young develop towards fledging, they begin to exercise their wings and spend some time up on the rim of the nest vibrating them rapidly. Eventually, they are coaxed away from the nest by the female, who can then continue to feed them on nearby perches.

The nestling period lasts for about 23 days in most species, but it could take a few days longer than this if the young experience difficult weather conditions and spend some time in torpor. The Andean hillstar has a nestling period that can be from 30 to 40 days long, so the whole nesting and brooding process can take as much as 60 days – over two months – during which time the female will have raised her young totally unaided by her mate.

Away from the nest too the female will continue to feed her young, and this period of dependency may last for a further 20 days or even longer. Black-chinned hummingbirds are fed by their mother for at least two weeks after leaving the nest, and in some tropical species this period of dependency may continue for a month after leaving the nest.

Many hummingbirds are double-brooded, so after a brief rest period the female will be attracted by a courting male, mating will take place, and the whole process will start again.

Some females have been known to go through the whole sequence of nest-building, egg-laying and incubation without having mated first. As a result, they lay infertile eggs which will not hatch. The may sit on them for several days longer than the normal in-cubation period, but they will eventually lose interest and abandon the nest.

It seems that only about 30 per cent of all broods are successfully raised, but although predators, bad weather and poor food supplies take their toll, the fact that most hummingbirds are double-brooded, coupled with their relatively long life-spans, enables them to maintain a high population.

Before they are ready to leave the nest, young hummingbirds exercise their wings; these Broad-tailed hummingbirds will soon be ready to fly.

CHAPTER 7

WHERE TO WATCH HUMMINGBIRDS

North America · Mexico

Guatemala · Costa Rica

Panama · The West Indies

Venezuela · Colombia

Ecuador · Peru · Chile

Argentina · Brazil

Surinam

The future for hummingbirds

Costa's hummingbird can be found in the south-western United States, especially in deserts where sages, Yuccas and Cholla cacti are plentiful.

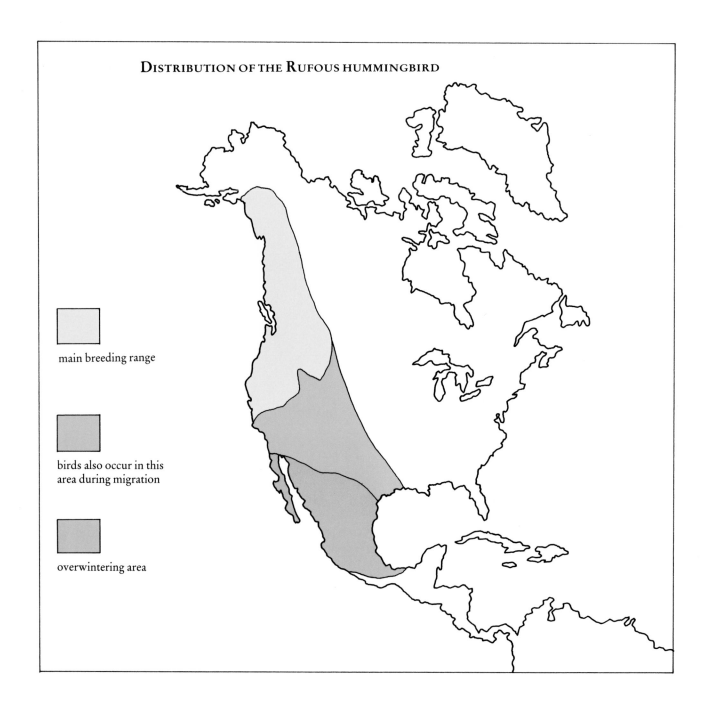

DISTRIBUTION OF THE RUFOUS HUMMINGBIRD

main breeding range

birds also occur in this
area during migration

overwintering area

By far the largest numbers of hummingbirds and the greatest variety of species are to be found in the equatorial regions of South America. Ecuador alone can boast over 120 species, but throughout North, Central and South America hummingbirds can be found in a great variety of habitats. From southern Alaska, where the Rufous hummingbird breeds in forests and thickets, to Tierra del Fuego, where the Green-backed firecrown nests, there will be hummingbirds breeding somewhere as long as there is a supply of nectar-producing plants and plenty of insects.

North America

Over the large part of the eastern United States and Canada the only species of hummingbird to be found is the Ruby-throated. It should not be too difficult to find as it favors areas with plenty of flowers, such as gardens and orchards. It seems to know no fear of man, so once spotted it can be fairly easily observed. Garden nectar feeders attract Ruby-throats, so there are many ways of seeing them at close quarters. During the winter months they will be absent from most of their breeding range. A few may overwinter in southern Florida, but the vast majority will be in Mexico and Central America, penetrating as far south as Panama.

More species of hummingbirds are present in the western states of the United States and Canada. The Rufous hummingbird breeds as far north as southern Alaska and can be found in pine and birch forests where there is a good variety of other flowering plants growing beneath the trees to provide the vital nectar. Many species of aphids breed in these forests, so finding insects in the northern summer is no problem. The bird is common on Vancouver Island, which provides good birdwatching generally. The tiny Calliope hummingbird can be found breeding in pine forests and mountain woodlands in several of the north-western states. It can be seen with the Rufous hummingbird in Yellowstone National Park in Wyoming.

Moving further south into California, with its warmer climate and wider variety of habitats and food plants, several new species are present, some remaining throughout the year. Both the Anna's and Costa's hummingbird can be found in the hills, and Anna's has often nested in suitable gardens. There is some movement to higher localities in the summer, so it may be necessary to travel to be able to find them, but during the winter they will both move to lower altitudes and will be found feeding on a variety of plants. Allen's hummingbird is common in brush and woodlands near the Californian coast, migrating there earlier in the spring and leaving sooner in the autumn than the very similar Rufous hummingbird. Griffith Park, about five miles north of Los Angeles, California, is a good site for seeing Anna's hummingbird, and in winter Allen's and Rufous hummingbirds can also be found there. The Tucker Bird Sanctuary in the Santa Ana mountains is worth a visit in July and August when the numbers of Anna's, Black-chinned, Rufous and Allen's hummingbirds are at a peak. The south-western states have the greatest variety of hummingbird species in the United States because of their proximity to Mexico, where many species breed.

The southern mountains of Arizona and New Mexico are worth exploring for species like the Black-chinned and Costa's, which nest where their food plants are common. Some are regular breeding species, but others are vagrants, being present in small numbers and perhaps not breeding every year. In these southern states there is always the chance of spotting a rarity that has strayed over the border from its southern nesting site. In summer the Broad-tailed and Rivoli's hummingbirds, and the Blue-throated mountain-gem breed in the higher hills and are fairly common, and there is a possibility of finding the Violet-crowned and White-eared hummingbirds as well.

MEXICO

Crossing the border into Mexico opens up a whole new world of opportunities for the keen birdwatcher, as the country boasts 51 species of hummingbirds, and they are widely distributed over a range of habitats. During the autumn migration the Yucatan peninsula receives migrant Ruby-throats from the United States across the Gulf of Mexico. The rainforest at Palanque is worth exploring for a variety of birds, including the Stripe-tailed hummingbird, Black-crested coquette, and Purple-crowned fairy. Other rarities include the Wedge-tailed sabrewing and the Fork-tailed emerald.

Western United States species move south from California to swell even further the numbers of passage migrants or overwintering birds. The rich forest of Singaita near San Blas, with its Gumbo limbo trees and palms, provides excellent birdwatching, and here one may glimpse the Long-tailed hermit. Many other species can be found and any suitable area of woodland with flowers blooming should be thoroughly searched.

Rivoli's hummingbird can be found in southern Arizona and Mexico, and also further south in Guatemala.

DISTRIBUTION OF THE RUBY-THROATED HUMMINGBIRD

main breeding range

birds also occur in this area, especially during migration

overwintering range – to arrive here, many birds face a long sea crossing

Gulf of Mexico

Yucatan Peninsula

The woods and hills around Mexico City hold many hummingbirds, and species such as the Fork-tailed emerald and the Berylline hummingbird may be found here. The tiny Bumble-bee hummingbird is rarer and may take some work to find.

GUATEMALA

The tropical forest of Tikal in Guatemala offers some of the finest birdwatching in Central America. It is relatively accessible, and there are forest walks which can be followed easily. A good selection of hummingbirds occurs in the forest, and observant visitors can expect to see the Long-tailed hermit, Scaly-breasted hummingbird, Wedge-tailed sabrewing, Green-breasted mango, Fork-tailed emerald, White-bellied emerald, Buff-bellied and Rufous-tailed hummingbirds, Black-crested coquette, Purple-crowned fairy, and White-necked jacobin. Several other species occur, and a few days could be spent here quite profitably.

Panajachel, on the shores of Lake Atitlan, the home of the rare flightless Atitlan grebe, is a good site for the Sparkling-tailed and White-eared hummingbirds, which feed in the gardens of hotels and villas. Various roads and trails lead up into the hills, and a further selection of hummingbirds may be found in the woods and clearings. Look out for the Red-billed azurecrown, and the Amethyst-, Wine- and Green-throated mountaingems. The Slender sheartail, which also occurs here, is rarer and much harder to find.

COSTA RICA

The further south one travels in Mexico and Central America, the more numerous the hummingbirds become. Costa Rica, a country only a fraction the size of Mexico, supports about 54 species of hummingbirds, which can be found breeding from sea level to around 10,000 feet (3000 m) up in the mountains. The country's many excellent national parks are helping to preserve vital habitats for them, and it is well worth trying to visit as many of the parks as possible. The Poas Volcan National Park is home to the endemic Cerise-throated hummingbird, as well as Rivoli's, or the Magnificent, and the Fiery-throated hummingbirds. The Monteverde National Park also supports interesting hummingbirds, but being a cloud-forest reserve it usually lives up to its name, and finding tiny birds in trees shrouded in mist can be quite a challenge. An information center in the park may offer some help and advice. The best time to visit is in the early morning, before the thick cloud has descended onto the hill tops.

Several species of hummingbird are common in upland areas, and species like the Green violet-ear and the Steely-vented hummingbird should be fairly easy to find. The Mangrove hummingbird is restricted to mangrove swamps and nearby bushy habitats on Costa Rica's Pacific coast, between the Gulf of Nicoya and the Golfo Dulce. Unfortunately, habitat destruction here is threatening the viability of the population of this very local bird.

PANAMA

The hills and woods of Panama on the western border with Costa Rica provide good birdwatching, and there are a number of roads into the hills around Volcan Barú. Several species of hummingbirds are found here, including the Snowy-breasted and Scintillant, which are quite common, and rarities such as the Costa Rican or Magenta-throated woodstar, Fiery-throated hummingbird, and Green-fronted lancebill. The Volcano hummingbird also occurs here. Panama City, or rather the gardens and wooded country in and around it, are also worth searching for hummingbirds. Long-tailed and Little hermits are common, and many others, such as the Black-throated mango, Blue-tailed emerald, Crowned woodnymph, White-veined plumeleteer, and Purple-crowned fairy also occur.

THE WEST INDIES

The many and varied islands of the West Indies (or the Greater Antilles) offer a number of endemic species, plus more widespread South American birds. Unfortunately, the political situation in some islands has made visiting them difficult at times. Cuba is the only site of the Bee hummingbird, which is becoming scarcer there; it lives in isolated areas in patches of woodland and scrub. However, many nature reserves have been established on the island, and it must be hoped that the future of the world's smallest bird is now more secure. The Vervain hummingbird, only a fraction larger than the Bee hummingbird, can be found on Haiti, along with the Antillean mango hummingbird, but habitat destruction is very severe here and the continued survival of the birds is questionable. The Hispaniolan emerald lives in what remains of natural woodland. The Dominican Republic has suffered less from habitat destruction, and finding some of the Antillean specialities may be easier here.

The Bahamas, not far to the east of Florida and north of Cuba offer a number of endemic birds, including the Bahama woodstar, which is quite common. The Cuban emerald also occurs here, and Ruby-throated hummingbirds from the mainland United States may pass through or overwinter.

Jamaica offers some very good birdwatching with a variety of habitats that are worth exploring. South of Montego Bay, at Anchovy, is the Rocklands Feeding Station where it should be possible to see the Streamertail and the Jamaican mango. Some natural woodland remains in Puerto Rico, such as at El Yunque, to the east of San Juan, the Luquillo Experimental Forest, and the Maricao State Forest. With some careful searching it should be possible to find the Puerto Rican emerald, the Antillean mango, the Green mango, the Green-throated carib, and the Crested hummingbird. The Virgin Islands have quite a rich bird life, which also includes the Crested hummingbird and the Green-throated carib.

The Lesser Antilles form a chain of islands stretching from Anguilla southwards towards

Grenada and the South American mainland. Many of the islands still have some tropical rainforest covering the higher hills, but this is disappearing at an alarming rate. Some of the islands are heavily used by tourists but others have escaped much development and still support a rich birdlife. The Purple-throated carib can be found in the forest on Boggy Peak on Antigua. On Guadeloupe the Crested hummingbird and Green-throated

The Green-throated carib can be found on Antigua and other neighboring Caribbean islands.

carib can be found near the capital Pointe-à-Pitre, while higher up in the forests lives the Purple-throated carib. Martinique has suffered badly from habitat destruction, and bird-trapping and shooting are rife among the local population. Nevertheless, it is still possible to find species such as the Blue-headed hummingbird in quieter areas. The island of Grenada is heavily cultivated, but the Rufous-breasted hermit can still be found here.

The islands of Trinidad and Tobago both offer good birdwatching in interesting

surroundings. Although there are no endemic species, there is a good selection of South American birds with plenty of hummingbirds. Rufous-breasted, Green and Little hermits are found on Trinidad, while other common species there are the Green-throated and Black-throated mangos, Tufted coquette, Blue-chinned sapphire, White-tailed goldenthroat, White-chested emerald, and Long-billed starthroat. The White-tailed sabrewing can only be found on the smaller island of Tobago, and it is rare there, but some species, like the White-necked jacobin and Copper-rumped hummingbird, occur on both islands.

VENEZUELA

The Henri Pittier or Rancho Grande National Park in Venuezuela supports one of the continent's best avifaunas. Many hummingbirds occur here and birdwatchers can profitably spend several days in the area, making daily trips into the park from Maracay. Weekends can be rather noisy as local people use the park then. In the higher ground of the park it is possible to see a great number of species, including the Brown and Green violet-ears, the Violet-headed and Violet-chested hummingbirds, Bronzy inca, Booted racket-tail, and the Long-tailed sylph. Lower down a number of rarities occur, but they are harder to find; the Lazuline sabrewing, Spangled coquette, and the Long-billed starthroat are present in scattered localities. The Blue-tailed and Glittering-throated emeralds should be easier to find in the lower hills of the park. The rainforest on the Paria Peninsula is one of the last strongholds of the endangered White-tailed sabrewing, which is surviving only where the rainforest has not been cleared. This forest is also the only site for the endemic Scissor-tailed hummingbird, which is greatly at risk from forest clearance.

COLOMBIA

Tayrona National Park on the coast of Colombia is a good birdwatching site as it offers numerous hummingbirds in addition to many other exciting South American bird species. The Pale-bellied hermit, Blue-tailed emerald, White-chinned sapphire, and Steely-vented hummingbirds are relatively common here. Also on the coast is the Isla de Salamanca National Park, which is much more of a wetland area. The Sapphire-bellied hummingbird is a rare species restricted to coastal mangroves near Cienago Grande and the Rancheria estuary; one of its few sites has already been destroyed by the construction of a pipeline. The San Lorenzo Ridge, south-east of Santa Marta, has a TV mast on it and is accessible by road. It is part of the Sierra Nevada de Santa Marta and provides access to hilly, wooded country where unusual species, such as the White-tailed starfrontlet and the Blossomcrown, occur. Many of the common species occur here also. The newly created Parque de los Farallones west of Cali in the western Andes has a very impressive list of

hummingbirds, and species such as the Tawny-bellied hermit, Brown, Green and Sparkling violet-ears, Andean emerald, Speckled hummingbird, Purple-bibbed whitetip, and Empress brilliant live here, but many others can be found if the area is thoroughly searched.

ECUADOR

The capital of Ecuador, Quito, is situated at 9300 feet (2800 m) above sea level and has an interesting variety of habitats in the city itself. Parks and gardens, and the remaining small areas of semi-natural woodland should be searched for species like the Black-tailed trainbearer, Sparkling violet-ear, and the Giant hummingbird. The Volcan Pichincha lies a short distance to the west of the city, and there is a road travelling a good part of the way up its slopes; the Speckled hummingbird may be found in the open woodland on the lower slopes, while higher up, at around 13,000 feet (4000 m), it should be possible to find species like the Sapphire-vented puffleg, Great sapphirewing, and Giant and Sword-billed hummingbirds. The Black-breasted puffleg is known only from the slopes of Volcan Pichincha and Volcan Atacazo, but it is endangered as habitat destruction close to the city is reducing its main breeding areas.

So many other species of hummingbirds are found in Ecuador that it is worthwhile

The Gould jewel-front is found in tropical forests from Venezuela to Brazil.

The Blue-chinned sapphire is a widespread but little known species of dark tropical forests in South America. It appears to be spreading to gardens and coffee plantations in areas where its natural habitat is declining.

searching in any habitat which provides flowers and insects. Generally, the higher, uncultivated ground is more productive, but many parks and gardens hold several species. Some hummingbirds are common in Ecuador and should not be too difficult to find; the Sparkling violet-ear, Shining sunbeam, Tyrian metaltail, and Collared inca are all quite widely distributed. A cruise on the Rio Napo aboard the floating hotel between Coca and Primavera, with forays into the forest and along the many backwaters, gives an opportunity to see some of the dense forest species of hummingbirds. Birdwatching can be difficult in densely vegetated areas, but the

The Buff-tailed coronet can be found in the highlands of the western Andes in Colombia and Ecuador.

local trained guides can be very helpful. The Rufous-breasted, Long-tailed, White-bearded, Straight-billed and Little hermits inhabit the forest, and among the other species living there are the Pale-tailed barbthroat, Grey-breasted sabrewing, Blue-tailed emerald, Fiery topaz, Golden-tailed sapphire, and Gould's jewelfront.

PERU

The mountainous country of Peru has a number of the more common hummingbirds as well as some endangered species. The city of Lima has some parks that are home to several hummingbirds, including the Amazilia. Other coastal towns that are less built up offer quite good birdwatching, and it should be possible to find the Oasis hummingbird, Purple-collared woodstar, and the Peruvian sheartail.

The ancient city of Cuzco lies high up in the Andes at about 11,400 feet (3500 m) above sea level and is a base for exploring the surrounding hills and valleys. The ruined Inca city of Machu Picchu is a great tourist attraction and is often very crowded, but there is plenty of good birdwatching to be done in the area, with many species of hummingbirds to find. The Buff-tailed sicklebill, Green-and-white and Speckled hummingbirds, Andean and Black-breasted hillstars, Giant hummingbird, Shining sunbeam, Chestnut-breasted coronet, and White-bellied woodstar all occur within sight of Machu Picchu.

The Royal sunangel is known with certainty only from the scrub-covered slopes below the forest and in the ravines of the Cordillera del Condor, Cajamarca, above the town of San Jose de Lourdes at about 6000

The large Stromelia flowers found high in the Andes in Peru offer valuable food for high altitude hummingbirds which usually perch whilst feeding.

feet (1800 m). The Neblina metaltail is restricted to low forest on the Cerro Chinguela in the Piura department. One of the rarest and most unusual of all hummingbirds is the Marvellous spatuletail, which sports incredibly long tail streamers formed from each outermost feather of the tail. It lives in montane scrub and along forest edges on the east side of the Utcubamba valley in southern Amazonas, and its habitat is under constant threat of destruction.

CHILE

The city of Arica and its surroundings on the coastal plain of Chile is the home of one of the most endangered of all hummingbirds. The Chilean woodstar seems to be entirely confined to man-made habitats in the city, such as gardens, and the cultivated valleys of the Azapa and Lluta rivers. The whole area is surrounded by some of the world's most arid deserts; only in a few remote valleys where rivers flow and plants flourish was there ever any suitable natural habitat for hummingbirds. The Chilean woodstar probably inhabited these valleys long ago before they were settled and cleared for agriculture. Gradually, isolated populations were wiped out until only a few birds remained in areas where suitable food plants existed. Only the man-made habitats now provide food for a much reduced population. The use of insecticides has severely depleted the supply of insect food available, and the replacement of native wild plants with agricultural crops has provided a poor alternative supply of nectar, so the birds are reduced in numbers and yet are still totally dependent on the man-made environment. Also living in Arica is the larger Oasis hummingbird, which at one time was difficult to find but is now much more common. It appears that the Oasis hummingbird has been able to adapt to the man-made environment much more easily than the Chilean woodstar, and as the population of one bird has declined, so the population of the other has increased. The Chilean Woodstar may also have a small population in southern Peru.

The Juan Fernandez Islands off the coast of Chile are home to the endemic Juan Fernandez firecrown. There is thought to be a population of less than 500 remaining on the islands, and urgent conservation measures are required to prevent a further decline. Santiago, the capital of Chile, is a good base for exploring the Pacific coast to the west and the Andes to the east. The area has a Mediterranean-type climate, yet within a relatively short distance are high snow-capped peaks, deep, wooded valleys, rivers rushing through gorges, and a fine coastline. The farming land around Concon, north of Valparaiso, can be explored, and here the patient birdwatcher may find the Giant hummingbird, while the Cerro la Campana National Park is a site for the Green-backed firecrown, among several other species. The White-sided hillstar is also common here.

The Stripe-breasted starthroat occurs in the lowlands of eastern Brazil.

ARGENTINA

Argentina supports fewer hummingbirds than many other South American countries as, being so far south, its climate is less favorable. The Green-backed firecrown breeds in the south of the country but migrates north for the winter. The Glittering-bellied emerald also occurs and can sometimes be found in the remaining areas of natural vegetation.

The Iguassu Falls, in the north of the country at the borders of Brazil, Argentina and Paraguay, offer good birdwatching against the spectacular backdrop of a vast waterfall. Extensive forests remain here, and national parks have been created in Argentina and Brazil to preserve some of the best habitats. Trails and boardwalks are being created, and hotels of various standards are already present. Finding small birds can be difficult in dense forest, but it should be possible to find the Scale-throated hermit, Black-throated mango, Glittering-bellied emerald, and the Violet-capped wood-nymph.

BRAZIL

In Brazil's Itatiaia National Park there are several hotels offering different standards of accommodation. The Hotel do Ipe has the added attraction of an array of hummingbird feeders in the gardens, and many species can be seen without leaving the grounds at all. Several woodnymphs and rubies visit frequently, and the White-throated hummingbird is a regular visitor, although about ten more species also appear from time to time. Several trails and roads lead off into the park itself, some reaching very high ground. Weekends in the summer can be crowded and noisy. Common hummingbirds in the park are the Scale-throated hermit and the Black jacobin, but the Swallow-tailed hummingbird and White-vented violet-ear also occur; the Planalto hermit is a local species which is more difficult to find.

The international resort of Rio de Janeiro with its high population, high prices and 24-hour a day way of life may seem an unlikely place for hummingbirds, but there are parks, botanical gardens, and wooded slopes surrounding the city. If it is possible to stay at the edge of the city and visit some of the quieter, well-vegetated areas, several species of hummingbirds may be seen, including the Reddish hermit, Black jacobin, Swallow-tailed hummingbird, Versicolored, Glittering-throated and Glittering-bellied emeralds, Violet-capped woodnymph, White-vented violet-ear, and the Black-bellied thorntail.

Belem is a city of about half a million people located near the mouth of the Amazon; it has several hotels and is a good base for exploring the lower Amazon. Many of the best birding areas require entry permits, which can be obtained in the city. The agricultural research organization called EMBRAPA should be able to help. Some of the remaining small areas of forest hold good numbers of hummingbirds, including some of the scarcer species, such as the Dot-eared coquette, Rufous-throated sapphire, and the Crimson topaz. Commonly occurring species include the White-necked jacobin, Common woodnymph, and the Black-eared fairy. Birdwatchers with a good head for heights may like to climb the 100-foot (30 m) high tower in the EMBRAPA research area. It allows a view down on to the tree canopy and an opportunity to see species normally out of view from birdwatchers at ground level. The Hyacinth visorbearer was once collected by the hundreds, but it is much more difficult to find now. It seems to be restricted to a few mountain ranges in north Minas Gerais, where it is protected to some extent in a national park and other reserves. The rare Hook-billed hermit can be seen in the CVRD Porto Seguro Reserve, which is one of its last strongholds. It was formerly widespread in lowland forests. The inland port of Manaus, 2000 miles (3200 km) from the sea and at the confluence of the Rio Negro and the

Tyrian metaltails are attracted to garden nectar-feeders in Brazil, and they are more inclined to perch whilst feeding than most other hummingbirds.

Solimoes, is at the start of the Amazon proper; at this point the river is already eight miles (13 km) wide. The grounds of the Hotel Tropicale provide a good habitat for hummingbirds, as they consist of remnants of the native forests and contain many suitable food plants. It should be possible to see several species here, including the Black-throated mango and Glittering-throated emerald. The grounds of the research institute INPA in Manaus also are good hummingbird habitat.

SURINAM

Surinam has preserved many of its lush tropical forests, and a number of them are now reserves. By contacting the government's forestry agency, STINASU, in Paramaribo, permits and information can be obtained. The Raleigh Falls Reserve and Foengoe Island on the Coppename River offer outstanding birdwatching, and the Brownsberg Reserve is situated to the west of the Afobaka dam on the Suriname River, where there is still some intact rainforest. Among the many species of hummingbirds that live here are the Rufous-breasted, Long-tailed, Straight-billed, Reddish and Little hermits, Green-throated and Black-throated mangos, Tufted and Racket-tailed coquettes, Rufous-throated and White-chinned sapphires, White-tailed and Green-tailed golden-throats, Glittering-throated and Plain-bellied emeralds, Crimson topaz, and Black-eared fairy.

THE FUTURE FOR HUMMINGBIRDS

In so many countries trapping, shooting, poisoning, and habitat destruction have led to the decline and even the total extinction of some hummingbird species, so it is to be hoped that if birdwatchers visit these countries and show that they are genuinely interested in seeing the birds thriving in their natural habitats, the authorities there may realize that they have a resource that must be preserved.

Previous generations treated the hummingbirds, along with many other species of birds, mammals and plants, as a resource to be plundered relentlessly; vast numbers of hummingbirds were taken simply to satisfy people's vanity. It could be argued that in the last century the ecology of tropical regions was not fully understood and that the trappers were quite unaware of the harm they were doing. We certainly cannot use that argument now as we have a very good understanding of the harm that has been done in the past and can see quite clearly what damage we are doing now, not just to the hummingbirds, but to the wider environment. It is our responsibility to ensure that these beautiful and fascinating birds survive long into the future so that following generations also can marvel at the living jewels of the air.

The Rose of Venezuela attracts hummingbirds to feed in the tree canopy. Observing a flower like this for some time is a good way of finding hummingbirds as they will pay frequent visits to collect nectar during the day.

Scientific names of hummingbirds

The following list contains the common English names and the scientific names of all species mentioned in the text. The names used follow those in the *Checklist of the Birds of the World* by Edward S. Gruson.

Allen's hummingbird	*Selasphorous sasin*	Blossomcrown	*Anthocephala floriceps*
Amazilia hummingbird	*Amazilia amazilia*	Blue-chested hummingbird	*Amazilia amabilis*
Amethyst-throated mountaingem	*Lampornis amethystinus*	Blue-chinned sapphire	*Chlorestes notatus*
Andean emerald	*Amazilia franciae*	Blue-headed hummingbird	*Cyanophaia bicolor*
Andean hillstar	*Oreotrochilus estella*	Blue-tailed emerald	*Chlorostilbon mellisugus*
Anna's hummingbird	*Calypte anna*	Blue-throated golden-tail	*Hylocharis eliciae*
Antillean mango	*Anthracothorax dominicus*	Blue-throated mountaingem	*Lampornis clemenciae*
Bahama woodstar	*Calliphlox evelynae*	Blue-throated sylph	*Aglaiocercus kingi*
Band-tailed barbthroat	*Threnetes ruckeri*	Booted racket-tail	*Ocreatus underwoodii*
Bearded helmetcrest	*Oxypogon guerinii*	Broad-tailed hummingbird	*Selasphorus platycercus*
Bee hummingbird	*Mellisuga helenae*	Bronzy inca	*Coeligena coeligena*
Berylline hummingbird	*Amazilia beryllina*	Brown inca	*Coeligena wilsoni*
Black-bellied thorntail	*Popelairia langsdorfii*	Brown violet-ear	*Colibrae delphinae*
Black-breasted hillstar	*Oreotrochilus melanogaster*	Buff-bellied hummingbird	*Amazilia yucatenensis*
Black-breasted plovercrest	*Stephanoxis lalandi*	Buff-tailed coronet	*Boissonneaua flavescens*
Black-breasted puffleg	*Eriocnemis nigrivestis*	Buff-tailed sicklebill	*Eutoxeres condamini*
Black-chinned hummingbird	*Archilochus alexandri*	Bumble-bee hummingbird	*Atthis heloisa*
Black-crested coquette	*Paphosia helenae*	Calliope hummingbird	*Stellula calliope*
Black-eared fairy	*Heliothryx aurita*	Cerise-throated hummingbird	*Selasphorous simoni*
Black jacobin	*Melanotrochilus fuscus*	Chestnut-breasted coronet	*Boissonneaua matthewsii*
Black-thighed puffleg	*Eriocnemus derbyi*	Chilean woodstar	*Eulidia yarellii*
Black-throated mango	*Anthracothorax nigricollis*	Chimborazo hillstar	*Oreotrochilus chimborazo*

Collared inca — *Coeligena torquata*
Colorful puffleg — *Eriocnemus mirabilis*
Costa Rican woodstar — *Philodice bryantae*
Costa's hummingbird — *Calypte costae*
Crimson topaz — *Topaza pella*
Cuban emerald — *Chlorostilbon ricordii*
Dot-eared coquette — *Lophornis gouldii*
Empress brilliant — *Heliodoxa imperatrix*
Fiery-tailed awlbill — *Avocettula recurvirostris*
Fiery-throated hummingbird — *Panterpe insignis*
Fiery topaz — *Topaza pyra*
Fork-tailed emerald — *Chlorostilbon canivetii*
Fork-tailed woodnymph — *Thalurania furcata*
Frilled coquette — *Lophornis magnifica*
Giant hummingbird — *Patagona gigas*
Glittering-bellied emerald — *Chlorostilbon aureoventris*
Glittering-throated emerald — *Amazilia fimbriata*
Glowing puffleg — *Eriocnemus vestitus*
Golden-tailed sapphire — *Chrysuronia oenone*
Gould's jewelfront — *Polyplancta aurescens*
Green-and-black streamertail — *Trochilus polytmus*
Green-and-white hummingbird — *Amazilia viridicauda*
Green-backed firecrown — *Sephanoides sephanoides*
Green-breasted mango — *Anthracothorax prevostii*
Green-fronted lancebill — *Doryfera ludoviciae*
Green hermit — *Phaethornis guy*
Green-tailed golden-throat — *Polytmus theresiae*
Green-tailed train-bearer — *Lesbia nuna*

Green-throated carib — *Sericotes holosericeus*
Green-throated mango — *Anthracothorax viridigula*
Green-throated mountain-gem — *Lampornis viridipallens*
Green violet-ear — *Colibri thalassinus*
Grey-breasted sabrewing — *Campylopterus largipennis*
Guy's hermit — *Phaethornis guyi*
Hairy hermit — *Glaucis hirsuta*
Hispaniolan emerald — *Chlorostilbon swainsonii*
Hoary puffleg — *Haplophaedia lugens*
Hook-billed hermit — *Ramphodon dohrinii*
Horned sungem — *Heliactin cornuta*
Hyacinth visorbearer — *Augastes scutatus*
Jamaican mango — *Anthracothorax mango*
Juan Fernandez firecrown — *Sephanoides fernandensis*
Lazuline sabrewing — *Campylopterus falcatus*
Little hermit — *Phaethornis longuemareus*
Loddigges' racket-tail — *(see Marvellous spatuletail)*
Long-billed starthroat — *Heliomaster longirostris*
Long-tailed hermit — *Phaethornis superciliosus*
Long-tailed sylph — *(see Blue-throated sylph)*
Lucifer hummingbird — *Calothorax lucifer*
Magenta-throated woodstar — *(see Costa Rican woodstar)*
Magnificent hummingbird — *(see Rivoli's hummingbird)*
Mangrove hummingbird — *Amazilia boucardi*
Marvellous spatuletail — *Loddigesia mirabilis*
Mountain avocetbill — *Opisthoprora euryptera*
Neblina metaltail — *Metallura odomae*
Oasis hummingbird — *Rhodopis vesper*
Olivaceous thornbill — *Chalcostigma olivaceum*
Pale-bellied hermit — *Phaethornis anthophilus*
Pale-tailed barbthroat — *Threnetes leucurus*

Peruvian sheartail	*Thamastura cora*	Shining sunbeam	*Aglaeactis cupripennis*
Plain-bellied emerald	*Amazilia leucogaster*	Slender sheartail	*Dorica enicura*
Planalto hermit	*Phaethornis preteri*	Snowy-breasted	
Puerto Rican emerald	*Chlorostilbon maugaeus*	hummingbird	*Amazilia edward*
Purple-backed	*Ramphomicron*	Sooty-capped hermit	*Phaethornis augusti*
thornbill	*microrhynchum*	Spangled coquette	*Lophornis stictolopha*
Purple-collared		Sparkling-tailed	
woodstar	*Myrtis fanny*	hummingbird	*Tilmatura dupontii*
Purple-crowned fairy	*Heliothryx barroti*	Sparkling violet-ear	*Colibri coruscans*
Purple-throated carib	*Eulampis jugularis*	Speckled	*Adelomyia*
Racket-tailed		hummingbird	*melanogenys*
coquette	*Discosura longicauda*	Steely-vented	
Red-billed		hummingbird	*Amazilia saucerottei*
azurecrown	*Amazilia cyanocephala*	Straight-billed hermit	*Phaethornis bourcieri*
Reddish hermit	*Phaethornis ruber*	Streamertail	(*see* Green-and-black
Rivoli's			streamertail)
hummingbird	*Eugenes fulgens*	Stripe-tailed	
Royal sunangel	*Heliangelus regalis*	hummingbird	*Eupherusa eximia*
Ruby-throated		Swallow-tailed	
hummingbird	*Archilocus colubris*	hummingbird	*Eupetomena macroura*
Rufous-breasted		Sword-billed	
hermit	*Glaucis hirsuta*	hummingbird	*Ensifera ensifera*
Rufous hummingbird	*Selasphorous rufous*	Tawny-bellied hermit	*Phaethornis*
Rufous-tailed			*syrmatophorous*
hummingbird	*Amazilia tzacatl*	Tufted coquette	*Lophornis ornata*
Rufous-throated		Turquoise-throated	
sapphire	*Hylocharis sapphirina*	puffleg	*Eriocnemus godini*
Sapphire-bellied		Tyrian metaltail	*Metallura tyrianthina*
hummingbird	*Lepidopyga lillae*	Versicolored emerald	*Amazilia versicolor*
Sapphire-throated		Vervain	
hummingbird	*Lepidopyga coeruleogularis*	hummingbird	*Mellisuga minima*
Sapphire-vented		Violet-capped	
puffleg	*Eriocnemis luciani*	woodnymph	*Thalurania glaucopis*
Scale-throated hermit	*Phaethornis eurynome*	Violet-crowned	
Scaly-breasted		hummingbird	*Amazilia violiceps*
hummingbird	*Phaeocroa cuvicrii*	Violet-headed	
Scintillant		hummingbird	*Klais guimeti*
hummingbird	*Selasphorus scintilla*	Violet-tailed sylph	*Aglaiocercus coelestis*
Scissor-tailed		Volcano	
hummingbird	*Hylonympha macrocerca*	hummingbird	*Selasphorous flammula*

Wedge-tailed sabrewing	*Campylopterus curvipennis*	White-tailed goldenthroat	*Polytmus guainumbi*
White-bearded hermit	*Phaethornis hispidus*	White-tailed sabrewing	*Campylopterus ensipennis*
White-bellied emerald	*Amazilia candida*	White-tailed starfrontlet	*Coeligena phalerata*
White-bellied woodstar	*Acestura mulsant*	White-throated hummingbird	*Atthis ellioti*
White-chested emerald	*Amazilia chionopectus*	White-throated mountaingem	*Lampornis castaneoventris*
White-chinned sapphire	*Hylocharis cyanus*	White-tipped sicklebill	*Eutoxeres aquila*
White-eared hummingbird	*Hylocharis leuchotis*	White-veined plumeleteer	*Chalybura buffonii*
White-necked jacobin	*Florisuga mellivora*	White-vented violet-ear	*Colibri serrirostris*
White-sided hillstar	*Oreotrochilus leucopleurus*		

BIBLIOGRAPHY

Davis, L. I. (1972) *A Field Guide to the Birds of Mexico and Central America.* University of Texas Press: Austin.

Greenewalt, C. H. (1960) *Hummingbirds.* Doubleday and Co.: New York.

Gruson, E. S. (1976) *A Checklist of the Birds of the World.* Collins: London.

Harrison, C. (1978) *A Field Guide to the Nests, Eggs and Nestlings of North American Birds.* Collins: London.

Johnsgard, P. A. (1983) *The Hummingbirds of North America.* Smithsonian Institute: Washington D.C.

National Geographic Society (1983) *A Field Guide to the Birds of North America.* National Geographic Society: Washington D.C.

Peterson, R. T. & Chalif, E. L. (1973) *A Field Guide to Mexican Birds.* Houghton Mifflin Company: Boston.

Rutgers, A. (1972) *Birds of South America.* St Martin's Press: New York.

Scheithauer, W. (1967) *Hummingbirds.* T. Y. Crowell & Co.: New York.

Skutch, A. F. & Singer, A. B. (1973) *The Life of the Hummingbird.* Vineyard Books: New York.

PHOTOGRAPHIC ACKNOWLEDGMENTS

Ardea London Limited: 35; Dennis Avon 18, 70; John S. Dunning 60, 75, 104; M. D. England 31, 37, 45, 88, 93; Kenneth W. Fink 28, 80, 81; François Gohier 14, 22, 69, 100; S. Maslowski 26; P. Morris 25; S. Roberts 52; Adrian Warren 24; – **Bruce Coleman Limited:** Des & Jen Bartlett 87, 94; Bob & Clara Calhoun 13, 15, 29, 30, 34, 38, 50, 56, 91; A. J. Deane 21; Michael Fogden 62, 65; Wayne Lankinen 9, 40 (upper & lower), 41, 42, 78; H. Rivarola 96; Leonard Lee Rue III 99; A. J. Mobbs 19, 32, 58, 59, 110, 115; Hans Reinhard 27; Rod Williams 73, 112; G. Ziesler 97, 113; – Eric & David Hosking 117; – **Frank Lane Picture Agency:** Ron Austing 6; Frank W. Lane 111; – **Nature Photographers Limited:** M. R. Hill 108; Paul Sterry 61, 85; – **NHPA:** E. A. MacAndrew 36, 119; – **Oxford Scientific Films:** John Cooke 2; Michael Fogden 63; Richard Foster 49; Stan Osolinski 76; Wendy Shattil & Bob Rozinski 82; Robert A. Tyrrell 12, 55.

INDEX

Page numbers in *italics* refer to illustrations